MASTERING SUPERVISORY EXCELLENCE

Practical Strategies for Effective Leadership

Elijah M. James, Ph. D.

Canadian Cataloguing in Publication Data

Elijah M. James

Mastering Supervisory Excellence: Practical Strategies for Effective Leadership

ISBN 978-1-0690086-8-8

EJ Publishing
663 White Plains Run
Hammonds Plain
Nova Scotia, Canada   B4B 1W7

This book is lovingly dedicated to my dear friend, the late Evans Hector, whose life was a testament to the art of exceptional supervision.

Through his unwavering dedication, wisdom, and compassion, he exemplified the principles expounded in this book. May his legacy inspire supervisors everywhere to lead with integrity and excellence.

Table of Contents

Preface 1

Acknowledgments 5

Part I: Foundations of Effective Supervision 7

Chapter 1: The Role of the Supervisor 9

Chapter 2: Essential Mindsets for Supervisory Success ..22

Chapter 3: Understanding Team Dynamics 29

Part II: Practical Skills for Everyday Supervision .. 39

Chapter 4: Effective Communication Techniques............41

Chapter 5: Setting Clear Expectations and Goals............50

Chapter 6: Time Management and Delegation.................58

Part III: Building and Leading High-Performance Teams.. 69

Chapter 7: Motivating and Engaging Your Team 71

Chapter 8: Performance Management and Feedback.......81

Chapter 9: Conflict Resolution and Problem-Solving.......89

Part Iv: Advanced Supervisory Practices 99

Chapter 10: Navigating Change and Managing Transitions 101

Chapter 11: Coaching and Developing Team Members.. 110

Chapter 12: Building Accountability and Ownership..... 116

Part V Practical Solutions To Common Supervisory Challenges **125**

Chapter 13: Managing Remote and Hybrid Teams 127

Chapter 14: Stress and Crisis Management 138

Chapter 15: Dealing with Difficult Personalities and Situations 146

Part VI Supervising In Special Situations **157**

Chapter 16: Supervising Technical and Highly Educated People 159

Chapter 17: Supervising in the Public Sector 167

Part VII Supervising For The Future **177**

Chapter 18: Ethical Supervision and Integrity in Leadership 179

Chapter 19: The Evolving Role of Supervisors in a Changing Workplace 188

Conclusion **199**

Appendices **203**

Appendix A: Sample Templates and Checklists 205

Appendix B: Recommended Resources for Supervisors . 217

Appendix C: Self-Assessment Questionnaire on Ethical Leadership 221

Appendix D: Glossary 223

PREFACE

The role of a supervisor is one of the most dynamic and demanding in any organization. Supervisors are the crucial link between organizational strategy and the workforce that carries it out, making their responsibilities both vital and complex. Yet, many individuals find themselves thrust into supervisory roles with little preparation or guidance. They are expected to manage people, solve problems, and deliver results—all while handling the ever-changing demands of the modern workplace.

It was with this reality in mind that *Mastering Supervisory Excellence* was conceived. This book is not merely a collection of theories or abstract ideas. Instead, it is a practical guide designed to equip supervisors with the tools, skills, and mindset needed to thrive in their roles and inspire excellence in those they lead.

Throughout my career, I've witnessed firsthand the transformative power of exceptional supervision. I've seen teams flourish under leaders who knew how to communicate effectively, address conflicts constructively, and foster a culture of accountability and respect. Conversely, I've seen teams falter because of a lack of clear direction, unresolved tensions, or leadership that failed to adapt to changing circumstances. These experiences have taught me that great supervision is not a matter of chance—it is a skill that can be learned, honed, cultivated, and mastered.

This book covers a broad spectrum of topics critical to supervisory success, from foundational principles like effective communication and time management to more advanced topics like crises management, managing remote teams, and ethical leadership. Each chapter includes practical applications and real-world examples to help you bridge the gap between theory and practice. The content is not only relevant to today's challenges but also forward-looking, preparing you for the trends and technologies that will shape the workplace of tomorrow.

More than just a handbook for supervisors, this book is a call to action. It invites you to see your role as a supervisor not as a mere job but as an opportunity to influence lives, drive meaningful change, and contribute to a thriving workplace culture. Supervisors are not just managers of tasks; they are leaders of people. This distinction is at the heart of *Mastering Supervisory Excellence.*

The True-False quizzes at the end of each part of *Mastering Supervisory Excellence* offer a quick and effective way to assess understanding and retention of key concepts. These quizzes challenge readers to critically evaluate statements, reinforcing their knowledge while helping to clarify any misconceptions.

The simplicity of the true-false format allows readers to reflect on their grasp of the material without feeling overwhelmed, making it an accessible and practical tool for self-assessment. By highlighting essential takeaways, these quizzes help supervisors apply the principles of excellence with greater confidence and precision.

I encourage you to approach this book as a companion on your journey of growth and leadership. Reflect on the insights presented, engage with the exercises, and consider how you can apply these principles to your unique context. Remember, excellence is not a destination—it is a continual pursuit.

As you embark on this journey, know that your efforts matter. Your dedication to becoming an exceptional supervisor has the power to inspire others, elevate performance, and create lasting positive change. You are not just building a career; you are building a legacy.

Thank you for choosing this book as a resource for your development. May it empower you to master the art of supervision and lead with confidence, integrity, and purpose.

ACKNOWLEDGMENTS

The journey of writing *Mastering Supervisory Excellence* has been one of collaboration, reflection, and inspiration. It would not have been possible without the support, insights, and encouragement of many remarkable individuals and organizations.

First and foremost, I want to express my deepest gratitude to the countless supervisors, managers, and leaders who shared their experiences, challenges, and successes with me. Your contributions have enriched this book and served as a testament to the power of excellent supervision.

To the dedicated employees with whom I have had the privilege of working over the years, thank you for teaching me the value of teamwork, trust, and authentic leadership. Your efforts and feedback have been instrumental in shaping my understanding of what truly works in the dynamic workplace environment.

I owe special thanks to my design team, led by Miss Koren Norton whose expertise and attention to detail ensured that this book remained both attractive and practical. Your input elevated every page, and your commitment to excellence matched the very essence of this book's mission.

To my family and close friends, your unwavering support and encouragement have been my anchor throughout this process. You reminded me to persevere during challenging moments and to celebrate the small victories along the way.

To the readers of this book—supervisors at every stage of their journey—thank you for your commitment to growth and for trusting this resource to guide you. Your dedication to your teams and organizations is what drives progress and excellence in the workplace.

Finally, I wish to acknowledge the ever-changing landscape of work and leadership that inspired this project. The rapid evolution of technology, diversity in the workplace, and new models of teamwork are challenging and exciting supervisors everywhere to step into their roles with greater skill and adaptability. It is my hope that this book will serve as a trusted companion as you address these changes and embrace your role as a leader.

To everyone who contributed to this book directly or indirectly, thank you for believing in the vision of *Mastering Supervisory Excellence*. This work is as much a reflection of your insights as it is mine, and for that, I am deeply grateful.

Elijah M. James

PART I
FOUNDATIONS
OF EFFECTIVE
SUPERVISION

CHAPTER 1
THE ROLE OF
THE SUPERVISOR

Chapter Overview

In any organization, the supervisor plays a pivotal role in ensuring that teams function smoothly, goals are met, and employees are supported in their development. Supervisors bridge the gap between frontline employees and upper management, turning organizational strategies into actionable plans on the ground. Their responsibilities, however, extend beyond mere task management—they are leaders, mentors, problem-solvers, and role models.

In this chapter, we'll explore the core responsibilities of a supervisor, the essential skills every supervisor needs, and some common misconceptions about the role.

Key Learning Objectives

By the end of this chapter, you should be able to:

1. Define the primary responsibilities and functions of a supervisor.

2. Recognize the unique role supervisors play in bridging organizational goals with team performance.

3. Understand the critical influence supervisors have on workplace culture and employee engagement.

4. Identify essential skills and qualities that enhance supervisory effectiveness.

5. Recognize how supervisors contribute to both team and organizational success.

Section 1:
Core Responsibilities of a Supervisor

Every supervisor must wear multiple hats, adapting to the varied needs of their team and the organization. Below are the primary responsibilities that define the role:

Figure 1.1 Responsibilities of the Supervisor

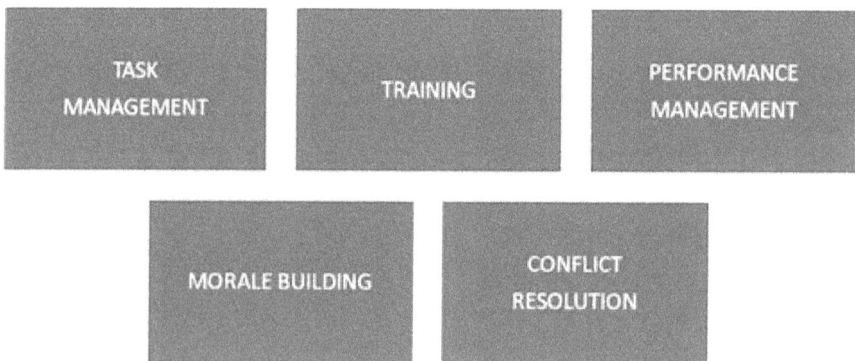

TASK MANAGEMENT

TRAINING

PERFORMANCE MANAGEMENT

MORALE BUILDING

CONFLICT RESOLUTION

1. Task Management and Delegation

Ensuring Team Productivity

Supervisors are responsible for ensuring that team members are productive and that projects are moving forward. This requires setting clear goals, establishing priorities, and tracking progress.

Effective Delegation

Rather than handling all tasks personally, supervisors need to delegate work in a way that maximizes the strengths of each team member. Effective delegation involves trusting your team members to handle their responsibilities while providing support as needed.

2. Training and Development

Skill Building

A supervisor's role includes helping team members develop their skills. This might involve on-the-job training, recommending professional development opportunities, or coaching.

Mentoring

Beyond skill-building, supervisors should be role models who guide employees in their professional growth, providing advice and helping them to deal effectively with challenges.

3. Performance Management

Setting Expectations

Supervisors must communicate expectations clearly and ensure that employees understand their roles and responsibilities.

Providing Feedback

Regular feedback, both positive and constructive, is essential for employee growth. Effective supervisors give feedback in a way that is specific, timely, and aimed at improvement.

Conducting Performance Reviews

Supervisors should conduct regular performance reviews to assess and discuss an employee's progress, identifying areas for improvement and acknowledging achievements.

4. Building Team Morale and Engagement

Fostering a Positive Work Environment

Team morale significantly impacts productivity and job satisfaction. Effective supervisors build a supportive, inclusive environment where employees feel valued.

Engaging and Motivating Team Members

Engaging employees goes beyond compensation; it involves recognizing achievements, aligning work with individual strengths, and creating a sense of purpose within the team.

5. Conflict Resolution and Problem-Solving

Managing Disagreements

Conflict is natural in any team setting, but it must be handled constructively. Supervisors play a key role in resolving conflicts, whether they arise between team members or within individual tasks.

Encouraging Problem-Solving

Supervisors should foster an environment where employees feel empowered to solve problems independently and collaboratively, with support available as needed.

The Supervisor's Job Description

We can learn much about the supervisor's role by examining the supervisor's job description below.

JOB TITLE: JANITORIAL SUPERVISOR

DEPARTMENT: OPERATIONS

REPORTS TO: OPERATIONS MANAGER

JOB(S) SUPERVISED: CLEANERS/JANITORS

JOB PURPOSE: MAINTAINS SAFE AND CLEAN
                     WORKING ENVIRONMENT
                     by
                     directing the work of cleaners.

ESSENTIAL JOB RESULTS:

1. DIRECTS CLEANING ACTIVITIES
   by
   assigning cleaning responsibilities.

2. SUPERVISES CLEANERS
   by
   checking work and requiring necessary corrections.

3. MAINTAINS WORKFLOW
   by
   ensuring that cleaning is completed in a timely manner.

4. MAINTAINS CLEANING STAFF

by

recruiting, selecting, orienting and training cleaning staff.

5. MAINTAINS CLEANING SUPPLIES INVENTORY

by

checking stock to determine inventory level; anticipating needed supplies; placing orders for supplies; verifying receipt of supplies.

6. CONSERVES CLEANING RESOURCES

by

using equipment and supplies as needed to accomplish job results; monitoring use by cleaners.

7. PREPARES REPORTS

by

collecting, analyzing, and summarizing information.

8. MAINTAINS CLIENT CONFIDENCE

by

keeping information confidential.

9. CONTRIBUTES TO TEAM EFFORT

by

accomplishing related results as needed.

Section 2:
Key Skills for Supervisory Success

To succeed in this multifaceted role, supervisors need a range of skills. Here are the core competencies that every effective supervisor should cultivate:

1. Communication Skills

Supervisors must communicate clearly and effectively, whether they are giving instructions, offering feedback, or discussing issues with employees. Active listening is equally important—it allows supervisors to understand employee concerns and respond appropriately.

2. Time Management and Organization

Balancing multiple responsibilities requires strong time management skills. Supervisors must organize their own time while helping team members prioritize their tasks to stay on track.

3. Empathy and Emotional Intelligence

Supervisors work with people, not machines. Empathy—the ability to understand and share the feelings of others—is essential for building trust and rapport. Emotional intelligence (the capacity to be aware of, control, and express one's emotions, and to handle interpersonal relationships judiciously and empathetically) helps supervisors recognize and manage their own emotions as well as the emotions of their team.

4. Adaptability and Problem-Solving

Supervisors must adapt to changing circumstances and find solutions to unexpected challenges. An adaptable supervisor stays calm under pressure and works proactively to resolve issues before they escalate.

Section 3: Common Misconceptions About Supervision

Misconception 1: Supervision is Only About Getting Results

Many assume that the primary role of a supervisor is to ensure productivity. While achieving results is crucial, effective supervision also involves supporting, motivating, and developing team members. It is easier to achieve productivity targets when employees are motivated.

Misconception 2: A Supervisor Must Always Have All the Answers

Some believe that supervisors need to have answers to every problem. It is true that supervisors should be well informed about certain things, but in reality, they are most effective when they leverage their team's knowledge, encourage collaborative problem-solving, and facilitate learning.

Misconception 3: Supervision is Just Another Step Up the Ladder

Many see supervision as a stepping stone in a career path, but it is much more than that. Effective supervisors are dedicated to their team's growth and success, and they recognize that supervision is a valuable, impactful role in its own right.

Section 4: The Supervisor's Role in Balancing People and Profit

A supervisor walks a fine line when balancing the well-being of team members with the need to achieve profitability. Leaning too far in one direction can lead to significant challenges for both the team and the organization.

The Consequences of Over-Prioritizing Employees

When a supervisor places excessive concern on workers at the expense of profits, the organization may face financial difficulties. This could happen if Resources are allocated beyond what the business can sustain, such as overly generous benefits or frequent rewards without corresponding performance gains. It could also happen if performance standards are relaxed to maintain employee comfort, potentially reducing productivity and overall output.

While this approach might foster short-term goodwill among employees, it risks the long-term viability of the business. Without sustainable profits, the organization may struggle to pay wages, invest in resources, or remain competitive, ultimately jeopardizing job security for everyone.

The Consequences of Over-Prioritizing Profits

Conversely, an excessive focus on profitability at the expense of employees can lead to a toxic work environment where workers feel undervalued and overburdened. This might manifest as high stress levels and burnout owing to unreasonable demands or lack of adequate resources; increased turnover as employees leave searching for workplaces that value their well-being; or decreased morale and engagement, leading to lower productivity and poorer quality outcomes.

Such an approach may yield short-term financial gains, but over time, it erodes the foundation of a thriving organization—its people. Workers who feel neglected or exploited are unlikely to perform at their best, and the costs of turnover and lost productivity can outweigh any immediate profit increases.

Finding the Equilibrium

A supervisor's success lies in balancing these two critical priorities:

For employees: Invest in their well-being, provide growth opportunities, and ensure they feel valued and heard.

For profits: Set clear expectations, monitor efficiency, manage resources wisely, and align employee goals with organizational objectives.

The following diagram illustrates the balance between concern for people and concern for profits.

Figure 1.2 Balancing Concern for People with Concern for Profits

This balance creates a virtuous cycle. Employees who feel cared for and empowered are more likely to deliver higher-quality work, driving profitability. Similarly, a profitable organization can invest more in its people, creating a sustainable, mutually beneficial dynamic.

By recognizing that the well-being of employees and the health of the organization are intertwined, a supervisor can navigate the challenges of leadership and create an environment where both workers and profits thrive.

Quick Tips for Defining Your Supervisory Role

Clarify Your Priorities

Identify the top three responsibilities that align most with your team's and organization's needs, and focus on excelling in these areas.

Develop a Leadership Statement

Write a short statement that captures your personal philosophy of supervision. This will guide your actions and keep you grounded in your values as a supervisor.

Regular Self-Reflection

Take time each month to evaluate your effectiveness as a supervisor. What's working well, and where can you improve? Continuous self-assessment is key to growth.

Key Takeaways

- **Supervisors Bridge Gaps:** They connect the organization's vision with day-to-day team operations.

- **Supervisors Shape Culture:** By setting the tone and modeling behavior, supervisors significantly influence workplace culture.

- **Effective Supervision Requires Balance:** Juggling administrative tasks with people management is crucial for a supervisor's success.

- **Success Depends on Development:** Supervisors are instrumental in nurturing team growth and aligning team members' development with organizational needs.

Real-Life Scenario: The First-Time Supervisor

Imagine Janet, a newly promoted supervisor in a mid-sized company. She's thrilled about her new role but quickly realizes the responsibilities are more complex than she anticipated. Her first challenge arises when two team members clash over a project approach. Janet initially hesitates, unsure of how to intervene, but remembers her role is to support both productivity and team harmony. She calls a meeting with both employees, listens to their perspectives, and guides them to a mutually agreeable solution. Janet's role in this situation is not just to "fix" the problem but to help her team learn constructive conflict resolution skills.

This example illustrates how supervisors often need to balance productivity with people management. Over time, Janet's supportive and proactive approach will foster a strong, collaborative team environment.

Self-Assessment Quiz

1. What do you consider the three most important responsibilities of a supervisor?

2. How would you handle a situation where two team members disagree on a project approach?

3. What are your strengths and areas for improvement as a supervisor?

Reflecting on these questions can help you better understand your approach to supervision and identify areas where you may want to focus as you continue reading.

CHAPTER 2
ESSENTIAL MINDSETS FOR SUPERVISORY SUCCESS

Chapter Overview

Make no mistake about it, the role of a supervisor is complex, requiring not only skills but also the right mindsets to lead teams effectively. In this chapter, we'll explore essential mindsets that successful supervisors embody. These mindsets help supervisors approach challenges positively, make informed decisions, and inspire their teams to reach their full potential. Developing these core mindsets will set you apart as a leader and create a strong foundation for supervisory success.

Key Learning Objectives

By the end of this chapter, you should be able to:

1. Understand the significance of a growth mindset and continuous improvement.

2. Embrace empathy and emotional intelligence in managing diverse teams.

3. Foster a mindset of accountability and ownership.

4. Recognize the importance of resilience and adaptability in a supervisory role.

5. Cultivate a proactive attitude toward problem-solving and team development.

Section 1: The Growth Mindset – Embracing Continuous Improvement

A growth mindset is the belief that skills, talents, and intelligence can be developed with effort and learning. Supervisors who adopt this mindset see challenges as opportunities rather than obstacles. This attitude not only helps you grow but also sets an example for your team, fostering a culture of learning and development.

Practical Steps

The following steps will help to develop a growth mindset:

Encourage Feedback: Regularly seek feedback from team members and peers to identify areas for improvement.

Set Development Goals: Create goals for your own professional growth as well as your team's.

Embrace Mistakes as Learning Opportunities: When mistakes happen, use them as opportunities to learn and improve processes.

Section 2: Empathy and Emotional Intelligence – Understanding Your Team

Empathy and emotional intelligence (EI) allow supervisors to connect meaningfully with team members, understanding their motivations, strengths, and challenges. By honing EI, you'll be better equipped to address interpersonal conflicts, provide support, and communicate effectively.

Practical Steps

Active Listening: Practice fully listening to team members without interrupting, and acknowledge their perspectives.

Recognize Emotions in Yourself and Others: Take time to identify and understand emotional responses, both yours and others', which can improve decision-making.

Support Individual Needs: Offer support and flexibility to accommodate personal and professional needs, which fosters trust and loyalty.

Section 3: Accountability and Ownership – Leading by Example

Supervisors who take accountability demonstrate responsibility for their actions and decisions, setting a standard for their team. Owning both successes and mistakes creates an environment where team members feel safe to take initiative and learn from their own experiences.

Practical Steps

Be Transparent About Decisions: Explain the reasoning behind your choices, especially when they affect the team.

Own Up to Mistakes: Acknowledge your own mistakes and demonstrate how to handle them constructively.

Set Clear Expectations and Follow Through: Clearly define team goals and make sure to provide the necessary support to meet them.

Section 4: Resilience and Adaptability – Staying Strong Through Change

Supervisors must be resilient and adaptable in order to deal with change and inspire their teams to do the same. These qualities allow you to manage setbacks calmly and adjust to new challenges without losing focus or confidence.

Practical Steps

Develop a Problem-Solving Attitude: When faced with challenges, focus on potential solutions rather than dwelling on obstacles.

Stay Calm Under Pressure: Practice techniques like deep breathing or mindful breaks to maintain composure during stressful situations.

Model Adaptability: Show your team that you can adjust to change by embracing new methods, tools, or workflows with a positive attitude.

Section 5: Proactive Leadership – Anticipating Needs and Challenges

Being proactive involves looking ahead, anticipating challenges, and taking steps to prevent or mitigate potential issues. A proactive mindset helps supervisors manage workloads more effectively, spot opportunities for improvement, and reduce the impact of unexpected situations.

Practical Steps

Plan Regular Check-Ins: Conduct regular team check-ins to address issues before they escalate.

Encourage Open Communication: Foster an environment where team members feel comfortable bringing up challenges and ideas.

Identify Areas for Process Improvement: Regularly evaluate workflows to find ways to increase efficiency and reduce friction points.

Reflection Questions

1. How do you currently approach challenges? Could adopting a growth mindset help you see them differently?

2. In what ways do you practice empathy and emotional intelligence with your team? Are there areas where you could improve?

3. Think of a recent mistake you made. How did you handle it? How might taking accountability have impacted your team's response?

4. Reflect on a time when you faced a significant change at work. What steps did you take to adapt, and how could you have modeled resilience for your team?

5. What proactive strategies do you currently use to manage team needs? Are there additional areas where a proactive approach could improve outcomes?

Key Takeaways

- **Growth mindset** fuels both personal and team development.

- **Empathy and emotional intelligence** strengthen relationships and enhance communication.

- **Accountability and ownership** build trust and set a standard of responsibility.

- **Resilience and adaptability** help supervisors and teams thrive through change.

- **Proactive leadership** enables supervisors to foresee and tackle issues before they arise.

Practical Application Exercise

Develop Your Supervisory Mindset Action Plan

1. Identify one mindset from this chapter that you would like to strengthen (e.g., resilience, empathy).

2. Write down one concrete action you'll take in the next week to work on this mindset.

3. Share your goal with a peer or mentor to increase accountability.

Example:

- *Mindset:* Accountability and Ownership
- *Action:* I will schedule weekly one-on-one check-ins to discuss my team's progress and challenges, allowing me to address any concerns directly and model accountability.

CHAPTER 3
UNDERSTANDING
TEAM DYNAMICS

Chapter Overview

Supervising a team requires more than just managing tasks; it involves understanding and fostering healthy team dynamics. In this chapter, we'll explore what makes teams function effectively, including the roles, relationships, and influences that affect team performance. By understanding these dynamics, supervisors can build trust, improve communication, and create a collaborative atmosphere where each team member feels valued and motivated.

Key Learning Objectives

By the end of this chapter, you should be able to:

1. Identify the key elements that influence team dynamics.

2. Recognize the roles and personalities that shape team interactions.

3. Build strategies for promoting trust and cooperation within your team.

4. Manage and leverage diversity within the team for enhanced performance.

5. Address common challenges in team dynamics, such as conflict and communication barriers.

Section 1:
The Building Blocks of Team Dynamics

Team dynamics are the unseen forces that shape how team members interact, communicate, and collaborate. Key factors influencing these dynamics include personalities, communication styles, cultural backgrounds, and the goals shared by the team. A strong supervisor understands these factors and works to harmonize them. The following diagram illustrates these key factors.

Figure 3.1 The Building Blocks of Team Dynamics

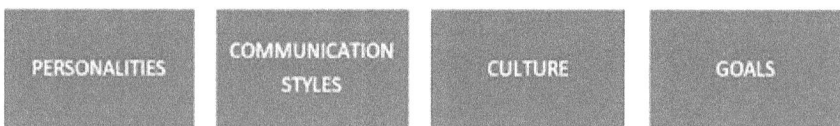

PERSONALITIES | COMMUNICATION STYLES | CULTURE | GOALS

Practical Steps

Assess Each Member's Strengths: Take time to learn about each team member's strengths, skills, and work preferences.

Define Clear Roles and Responsibilities: Ensure everyone understands his/her role and how it contributes to the team's objectives.

Establish Team Norms: Set ground rules for communication, meeting conduct, and decision-making to encourage consistency and fairness.

Section 2: Recognizing Individual Roles and Personalities

Every team consists of individuals with unique personalities and natural roles they tend to take on, such as leaders, supporters, innovators, and analysts. Understanding these roles can help you assign tasks more effectively and prevent misunderstandings.

Practical Steps

Identify Natural Strengths: Observe each person's contributions and tendencies, and consider these when delegating tasks.

Balance Task Assignments: Ensure tasks play to each member's strengths, avoiding overloading one individual or role.

Promote Inclusivity: Encourage each team member to contribute ideas, creating a balanced space where all voices are heard.

Section 3: Fostering Trust and Cooperation

Trust is the foundation of any successful team. When team members trust each other, they are more willing to collaborate, take risks, and support each other. As a supervisor, you set the tone for trust within your team.

Practical Steps

Model Transparency: Share relevant information openly and encourage others to do the same.

Encourage Open Feedback: Create a safe space for constructive feedback to improve teamwork and processes.

Recognize and Reward Team Efforts: Celebrate both individual and group achievements to reinforce the value of collaboration.

Section 4: Leveraging Diversity for Enhanced Performance

Diverse teams bring a range of perspectives, skills, and ideas that can lead to more innovative solutions. However, diversity can also lead to misunderstandings or conflict if not managed well. Embracing diversity can be a powerful asset to your team's success.

Practical Steps

Highlight the Value of Different Perspectives: Encourage team members to share their unique viewpoints and respect others' input.

Provide Cultural Awareness Training: Offer training sessions to help team members appreciate and understand diverse backgrounds and perspectives.

Celebrate Diversity: Acknowledge and celebrate the diverse strengths of your team through team-building activities or discussions that highlight these differences as assets.

Section 5: Addressing Common Challenges in Team Dynamics

Even in the best teams, challenges such as conflict, communication issues, and resistance to change can arise. Understanding how to address these challenges constructively is key to maintaining healthy team dynamics.

Practical Steps

Conflict Resolution Protocols

Establish clear guidelines for addressing conflicts, focusing on respectful and constructive conversations.

Adapt Communication Styles

Be flexible in your communication approach to ensure all members understand and are engaged.

Encourage a Growth Mindset

Remind team members that challenges are opportunities for growth, reinforcing a positive, solutions-oriented approach.

Reflection Questions

1. How well do you know your team members' individual strengths and personalities? Are there steps you can take to deepen this understanding?

2. In what ways do you currently promote trust within your team? Can you think of new methods to strengthen it?

3. How does your team handle diversity and differing viewpoints? Are there areas where acceptance and appreciation could be improved?

4. Think of a recent conflict or challenge your team faced. How did you handle it, and what might you do differently next time?

5. What new strategies could you implement to address common team challenges and improve team dynamics?

Key Takeaways

- **Understanding team dynamics** is essential for building a cohesive and productive team environment.

- **Recognizing individual roles and personalities** allows supervisors to leverage each member's strengths effectively.

- **Trust and cooperation** are foundational elements that drive team success and should be continuously nurtured.

- **Diversity within a team** can be a powerful asset if managed with respect and inclusivity.

- **Addressing challenges proactively** keeps team dynamics positive and helps prevent minor issues from escalating.

Practical Application Exercise

Create a Team Dynamics Action Plan

1. Identify one specific area of team dynamics you'd like to improve (e.g., enhancing trust, addressing communication gaps).

2. Write down three actionable steps you will take over the next month to address this area.

3. At the end of the month, evaluate the impact of these steps with your team and note any changes in team dynamics.

Example:

- *Focus Area:* Building Trust
- *Steps:*

  o Hold weekly team check-ins focused on open communication and idea sharing.

  o Schedule one-on-one meetings to learn more about each member's career goals and challenges.

  o Recognize team efforts at the end of each month, highlighting contributions and progress.

QUIZ FOR PART I

Indicate whether the following statements are true (T) or false (F).

1. A supervisor's responsibility is to make sure the work gets done. It has nothing to do with training   T   F

2. Emotional Intelligence (EI) is important for social workers, not for supervisors. T   F

3. The Supervisor must balance concern for people with concern for profits.   T   F

4. The belief that skills, talents, and intelligence can be developed with effort and learning is called a curious mindset.   T   F

5. Proactive leadership enables supervisors to foresee and tackle issues before they arise.   T   F

6. Cooperation, not trust, is a fundamental element that drives team success.   T   F

7. In supervising, diversity should be discouraged at all costs. T   F

8. Resilience and adaptability help teams thrive through change. T   F

9. Supervisors should never acknowledge their mistakes because their team members will think less of them. T   F

10. Supervisors don't get involved with recruiting and orienting, they supervise.   T   F

ANSWERS

1 F   2 F   3 T   4 F   5 T   6 F   7 F   8 T
9 F   10 F

PART II
PRACTICAL SKILLS
FOR EVERYDAY
SUPERVISION

CHAPTER 4
EFFECTIVE COMMUNICATION TECHNIQUES

Chapter Overview

Communication is the cornerstone of effective supervision. A supervisor's ability to convey ideas clearly, listen actively, and address misunderstandings can make or break team cohesion. This chapter will explore communication strategies that build trust, clarity, and mutual respect. Supervisors who master these techniques create an environment where ideas can flourish, challenges are addressed collaboratively, and feedback is exchanged openly.

Key Learning Objectives

By the end of this chapter, you should be able to:

1. Understand the importance of clarity and precision in all forms of communication.

2. Use active listening to foster trust and encourage open dialogue.

3. Communicate feedback constructively to drive improvement and morale.

4. Adapt communication styles to meet the needs of diverse team members.

5. Avoid common communication pitfalls that can lead to misunderstandings.

Section 1: Clarity and Precision in Communication

Effective supervisors communicate clearly and concisely, ensuring that their messages are understood without ambiguity. Clear communication not only prevents errors but also promotes confidence within the team. This is especially important in written instructions, performance expectations, and task assignments.

Practical Steps

Be Direct: State your purpose up front and avoid unnecessary jargon. Simplicity is key.

Repeat and Confirm: Restate key points at the end of a conversation and encourage questions to ensure clarity.

Use Visual Aids: When explaining complex tasks, use charts, diagrams, or written outlines to support your points.

A Simple Communication Model

A communication model illustrates how information flows between individuals or groups. Here is a straightforward and effective model with five core components.

1. Sender

The sender is the person or group initiating the communication. The sender has a message or idea to convey. He or she encodes the message making it clear.

2. Message

The message is the information, idea, or feeling the sender wants to communicate. For example, "Our goal is to increase productivity by 10% this quarter."

3. Channel

The channel is the medium through which the message is delivered. Channels include verbal (meetings, phone calls, and video conferences), non-verbal (body language, facial expressions), and written (emails, reports, and memos). The sender should try to use the most effective channel depending on the context. For example, a face-to-face meeting could be most appropriate for complex discussions.

4. Receiver

The receiver is the person or group for whom the message is intended. The key role of the receiver in this process is to decode and interpret the message accurately.

5. Feedback

Feedback is the receiver's response to the message, closing the communication loop. The key role of the receiver in this process is to ensure the sender knows whether the message was understood.

The Process Flow

The following outlines the communication flow from the sender to the receiver and back to the sender.

1. The **Sender encodes** a message.

2. The message is sent through an appropriate **channel**.

3. The **receiver decodes** the message.

4. The receiver provides **feedback** to confirm understanding or request clarification.

Example Scenario

Sender: A supervisor (explaining a change).
Message: "The delivery date has been changed from December 15 to November 30."
Channel: A team meeting for direct interaction and discussion.
Receiver: Team members.
Feedback: Team members respond with questions and suggestions

By focusing on clear encoding, appropriate channels, and active feedback, this simple communication model ensures effective and meaningful exchanges in any setting.

Section 2: Active Listening as a Supervisory Tool

Active listening is more than hearing words; it involves focusing fully on the speaker, showing empathy, and responding thoughtfully. When supervisors practice active listening, they gain valuable insights into their team's needs, concerns, and motivations.

Practical Steps

Show You're Engaged: Use verbal nods, maintain eye contact, and avoid distractions like checking your phone.

Ask Open-Ended Questions: Encourage your team members to share more by asking questions that can't be answered with a simple "yes" or "no."

Paraphrase and Reflect: Restate what the speaker has said in your own words to show understanding and allow clarification where necessary.

Section 3: Giving Constructive Feedback

Feedback is one of the most powerful tools in a supervisor's toolkit. When done well, it motivates, guides improvement, and fosters a growth mindset. Effective supervisors know how to provide feedback in a way that supports development without discouraging team members.

Practical Steps

Be Specific: Describe exactly what the team member did well or where he/she needs improvement, rather than using vague comments.

Balance Positive and Corrective Feedback: Start with positive feedback to set a constructive tone, then offer areas for improvement.

Offer Solutions, Not Just Criticism: Provide actionable steps for improvement to make feedback constructive rather than merely critical.

Section 4: Adapting Communication Styles for a Diverse Team

Team members bring varied backgrounds, communication preferences, and personalities to the workplace. Adapting your communication style to meet the needs of each individual is essential for inclusive and effective supervision.

Practical Steps

Identify Communication Preferences: Some people prefer written instructions, while others thrive on face-to-face communication. Observe and ask about each team member's preference.

Adjust Your Tone and Approach: Be aware of cultural and personality differences. While some team members respond well to a direct approach, others may prefer a gentler, more supportive tone.

Provide Multiple Communication Channels: Ensure important messages are shared both verbally and in writing to accommodate diverse preferences and reduce misunderstandings.

Section 5: Avoiding Common Communication Pitfalls

Ineffective communication can lead to misunderstandings, decreased morale, and conflict.

Recognizing and avoiding common pitfalls helps supervisors maintain clarity, respect, and productivity within their teams.

Practical Steps

Avoid Assumptions: Don't assume that a team member understands your instructions—always double-check and clarify.

Resist Interrupting: Let team members finish speaking before responding. This shows respect and helps you gather all relevant information.

Minimize Technical Jargon: Use plain language, especially when explaining new tasks or procedures, to avoid confusion and increase understanding.

Reflection Questions

1. Think about a recent conversation with a team member. How could active listening have enhanced the exchange?

2. When giving feedback, do you typically balance positive and corrective comments? How might this approach affect team morale?

3. Reflect on a time when a team member misunderstood your instructions. What steps can you take to prevent similar misunderstandings in the future?

4. How might you better adapt your communication style to accommodate the diversity within your team?

5. Are there common pitfalls in your communication style that you could work on to improve your interactions?

Key Takeaways

- **Clarity in communication** reduces misunderstandings and builds trust within the team.

- **Active listening** fosters an open and collaborative environment where team members feel valued.

- **Constructive feedback** supports personal and professional growth when delivered with respect and actionable suggestions.

- **Adapting communication styles** to team members' preferences enhances inclusivity and understanding.

- **Avoiding common communication pitfalls** keeps interactions respectful and productive.

Practical Application Exercise

Create a Personal Communication Plan

1. **Identify an area for improvement:** Review the key concepts in this chapter and select one communication technique you want to focus on (e.g., active listening, adapting styles, clarity in feedback).

2. **Set a short-term goal:** Define how you will incorporate this technique in your daily interactions over the next week.

3. **Evaluate progress:** At the end of the week, reflect on how this change has impacted your team's interactions and note any improvements or challenges.

Example:

- *Focus Area:* Giving Constructive Feedback

- *Goal:* During one-on-one meetings, begin feedback sessions by highlighting a specific accomplishment, then discuss an area for improvement with actionable suggestions.

- *Reflection:* Record responses from team members, noting how this balanced approach affects their motivation and response to feedback.

CHAPTER 5
SETTING CLEAR EXPECTATIONS AND GOALS

Chapter Overview

Setting clear expectations and achievable goals is essential for guiding team performance and maintaining a motivated workforce. Supervisors who clarify what's expected foster a productive, goal-oriented environment. This chapter explores techniques for setting expectations, defining meaningful goals, and ensuring team alignment with organizational priorities. By mastering these skills, supervisors empower their teams to work efficiently and contribute purposefully to the company's success.

Key Learning Objectives

By the end of this chapter, you should be able to:

1. Understand the importance of clarity when setting expectations for team members.

2. Establish achievable and measurable goals that align with organizational objectives.

3. Use goal-setting frameworks like SMART (Specific, Measurable, Achievable, Relevant, Time-bound) to ensure clarity and focus.

4. Communicate expectations in a way that encourages accountability and ownership.

5. Recognize and address barriers to achieving goals within the team.

Section 1: Importance of Setting Clear Expectations

Unclear expectations lead to confusion, errors, and reduced motivation. When team members understand precisely what is expected of them, they can approach their tasks with confidence, knowing their work contributes to larger goals. Clarity in expectations also reduces unnecessary oversight, allowing supervisors to focus on higher-level tasks while trusting their teams to perform reliably.

Practical Steps

Define Each Role: Outline responsibilities and key tasks associated with each role in your team.

Clarify Standards: Specify quality standards and timelines for each task to reduce ambiguity.

Explain the Why: When team members understand the purpose of their tasks, they are more likely to take ownership and work efficiently.

Section 2: Setting Effective Goals

Goal-setting provides direction, keeps teams focused, and encourages progress. Effective supervisors set goals that are both challenging and attainable, motivating team members to push their boundaries while keeping them from feeling overwhelmed.

Practical Steps

Use SMART Goals: Make sure each goal is:

Specific: Clearly define what you want to accomplish.

Measurable: Establish criteria to measure progress and success.

Achievable: Ensure the goal is realistic given the team's resources and abilities.

Relevant: Align the goal with broader organizational priorities.

Time-bound: Set a clear deadline for completion.

The following diagram illustrates these desirable features of goals.

Figure 5.1 Desirable Features of Goals

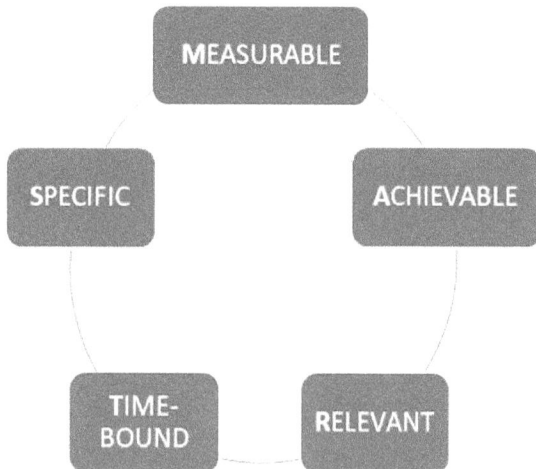

Involve the Team in Goal Setting: When team members participate in setting goals, they are more likely to be committed and motivated to achieve them.

Break Down Big Goals: Divide complex objectives into smaller, manageable tasks, providing a clear path to completion.

Section 3: Communicating Expectations Effectively

Clear, direct communication is critical for setting expectations that team members can understand and follow. Supervisors need to ensure that their expectations are conveyed in a way that team members find relatable and actionable.

Practical Steps

Use Clear Language: Avoid jargon or vague statements; be precise and direct.

Provide Examples: When possible, show examples of completed work that meets your expectations.

Confirm Understanding: Ask team members to restate their understanding of the expectations to ensure clarity.

Document Expectations: Put expectations in writing—this could be through email, shared documents, or team notes—so team members have a point of reference.

Section 4: Encouraging Accountability and Ownership

When team members take ownership of their work, they are more likely to perform consistently and take pride in meeting expectations. Supervisors play a key role in fostering this sense of accountability.

Practical Steps

Set Clear Consequences and Rewards: Let team members know the outcomes of meeting or missing goals to emphasize the impact of their efforts.

Empower Decision-Making: Give team members the authority to make decisions within their roles. This builds ownership and accountability.

Regularly Review Progress: Hold one-on-one and team meetings to check progress on goals and provide feedback, ensuring that everyone stays on track and can address any obstacles.

Section 5: Addressing Challenges in Goal Achievement

Challenges are inevitable in any goal-setting process. Effective supervisors anticipate potential barriers and work collaboratively with their teams to overcome them.

Practical Steps

Identify Potential Obstacles Early: Discuss possible challenges with your team at the outset to prepare solutions.

Adjust Goals as Necessary: Be willing to modify goals if circumstances change, ensuring they remain realistic and achievable.

Offer Support and Resources: Provide any necessary tools, training, or support that team members need to accomplish their tasks.

Encourage a Growth Mindset: Remind your team members that challenges are part of the growth process. Encourage them to view obstacles as learning opportunities rather than setbacks.

Reflection Questions

1. Think of a time when expectations were unclear. How did it affect your ability to perform? What could have been done differently?

2. Reflect on a goal you set recently. Was it SMART? If not, how could you adjust it to meet the SMART criteria?

3. How do you currently communicate expectations to your team? Are there ways you could enhance clarity and understanding?

4. What strategies do you use to encourage ownership among team members?

5. How do you handle unexpected challenges that arise during the pursuit of team goals?

Key Takeaways

- **Setting clear expectations** empowers team members to work with confidence and clarity.

- **Effective goals** are challenging but achievable, guiding team members toward meaningful accomplishments.

- **SMART goals** provide a structured approach to setting and achieving objectives.

- **Communication of expectations** is critical to avoid misunderstandings and maintain accountability.

- **Anticipating challenges** and working collaboratively with your team to overcome them foster resilience and adaptability.

Practical Application Exercise

Develop and Implement a Team Goal

1. **Identify a Team Objective:** Choose an area in your team's work that could benefit from a focused goal.

2. **Create a SMART Goal:** Define this objective in SMART terms to provide clarity and focus.

3. **Communicate the Goal to Your Team:** Clearly outline the goal, timelines, and each member's role.

4. **Monitor and Adjust as Needed:** Check in regularly to review progress and make adjustments based on any new developments or challenges.

Example:

- *Objective:* Improve customer response time by 20% over the next quarter.

- *SMART Goal:* "By the end of Q1, reduce our average customer response time from 48 hours to 38 hours through streamlined workflows and prioritization."

- *Communication:* Outline steps, assign specific roles, and schedule weekly check-ins to track progress.

CHAPTER 6
TIME MANAGEMENT
AND DELEGATION

Chapter Overview

Time management and delegation are two of the most essential skills for successful supervisors. Effective time management helps supervisors stay organized, focused, and productive, while delegation allows them to leverage their team's strengths, enhance efficiency, and build trust. In this chapter, we explore strategies and tools for optimizing time and delegating tasks effectively to promote a balanced, productive work environment.

Key Learning Objectives

By the end of this chapter, you should be able to:

1. Recognize the importance of prioritizing tasks and organizing time to boost productivity.

2. Identify techniques for creating a structured, time-efficient workday.

3. Develop skills in delegating tasks in a way that empowers team members and ensures accountability.

4. Recognize common obstacles to effective time management and delegation, and learn strategies to overcome them.

5. Apply practical tools for tracking progress and managing workload.

Section 1: The Importance of Time Management in Supervision

Supervisors are responsible for their own productivity and that of their teams, making time management essential to both personal success and team effectiveness. Efficient time management allows supervisors to focus on high-impact tasks, address team needs promptly, and maintain a steady workflow.

Practical Steps

Set Clear Priorities: Start each day by identifying the top three tasks that must be completed. Focus on these first to prevent minor tasks from consuming too much of your time.

Use a Planning Tool: Utilize digital calendars, task management apps, or physical planners to organize your day and keep track of deadlines.

Schedule Focus Time: Designate blocks of uninterrupted time for high-priority tasks, reducing the impact of distractions and interruptions.

Section 2: Structuring Your Workday for Maximum Efficiency

Organizing your day with a structured plan improves focus and helps prevent overwhelm. By creating a routine and managing your workload systematically, you can address tasks more effectively and ensure that nothing important is overlooked.

Practical Steps

Break Down Large Tasks: Divide complex projects into smaller, manageable steps. Tackling one step at a time prevents feeling overwhelmed and ensures steady progress.

Use the Two-Minute Rule: If a task takes two minutes or less, complete it immediately. This prevents small tasks from accumulating and cluttering your schedule.

Allocate Time for Routine Tasks: Schedule specific times for recurring tasks (e.g., checking emails) rather than handling them throughout the day. This approach reduces distractions and improves productivity.

Section 3: Understanding When and How to Delegate

Delegation is a core supervisory skill that involves assigning tasks to team members based on their strengths, skills, and development needs. Effective delegation frees up time for supervisors to focus on high-level responsibilities and fosters team growth. It also develops team members' confidence.

Practical Steps

Identify Delegable Tasks: Determine which tasks you can delegate without compromising quality or efficiency. Routine, time-consuming, or developmental tasks are often ideal for delegation.

Match Tasks with Team Members: Delegate tasks to individuals whose skills and experience align with the task requirements. For developmental tasks, consider assigning them to team members who would benefit from the learning opportunity.

Communicate Clear Expectations: When delegating, explain the task, its purpose, deadlines, and expected outcomes clearly. This ensures that the team member knows exactly what to accomplish and feels confident in his/her role.

These three steps are illustrated below.

Figure 6.1 Steps in Delegation

Identify task to be delegated

Match task with team members

Communicate clear expectations

Section 4: Building Trust and Accountability Through Delegation

Delegation is also a valuable tool for fostering trust and accountability within the team. By entrusting team members with responsibilities, supervisors show confidence in their abilities, which boosts morale and engagement.

Practical Steps

Empower Decision-Making: Allow team members some autonomy in handling delegated tasks, making them feel more accountable and invested in the outcome.

Provide Support, Not Micromanagement: Offer guidance and be available to answer questions, but avoid excessive oversight. This balance encourages independence and problem-solving skills.

Recognize Contributions: Acknowledge team members' efforts and successes. Showing appreciation motivates them to take ownership of future delegated tasks.

Section 5: Overcoming Common Challenges in Time Management and Delegation

Supervisors often face obstacles when trying to manage their time or delegate effectively. Identifying these challenges and developing strategies to address them can enhance productivity and prevent burnout.

Practical Steps

Combat Procrastination: Break large or intimidating tasks into small, manageable steps. Set short deadlines to create urgency and increase momentum.

Avoid Overloading Yourself: Learn to say no when your plate is full. Delegate tasks when appropriate and communicate your workload to upper management if necessary.

Handle Resistance to Delegation: If team members are hesitant to take on new responsibilities, provide reassurance and offer training or guidance to build their confidence.

Section 6: Tools and Techniques for Effective Time Management and Delegation

Using the right tools can streamline time management and make delegation smoother. Technology, task management systems, and organizational strategies can help supervisors keep track of multiple priorities.

Practical Steps

Task Management Software: Tools like Asana, Trello, or Microsoft Teams can help assign, track, and manage tasks across the team.

The Eisenhower Matrix: This decision-making tool categorizes tasks based on urgency and importance, helping you prioritize more effectively. The matrix below shows that tasks that are both important and urgent will be done first; those that are important but not urgent can be scheduled; those that are not important but urgent can be delegated; and those that are neither important nor urgent can be deleted.

Figure 6.2 The Eisenhower Matrix

Time Blocking: Use time blocks in your calendar for focused work, meetings, and breaks, ensuring a balanced and productive day.

Reflection Questions

1. Do you find it easy to manage your time as a supervisor? What areas could be improved?

2. Reflect on your current delegation practices. Are there tasks you could delegate more effectively?

3. Have you ever experienced burnout because of poor time management? What could have prevented it?

4. What steps could you take to make your workday more structured and efficient?

5. Are there additional tools or strategies you'd like to try to improve time management and delegation?

Key Takeaways

- **Effective time management** is foundational for supervisors to achieve their goals and lead their teams efficiently.

- **Structured workdays** prevent overwhelm, ensure focus on priorities, and enhance productivity.

- **Delegation empowers** team members by building trust, enhancing skills, and fostering accountability.

- **Addressing common challenges** in time management and delegation can improve efficiency and prevent burnout.

- **Utilizing the right tools** helps streamline time management and simplifies delegation, making both processes more effective.

Practical Application Exercise

Create a Delegation Plan

1. **Identify a Task to Delegate:** Choose a task you frequently handle that could be assigned to a team member.

2. **Choose the Right Person:** Select a team member whose skills align with the task.

3. **Set Expectations:** Outline the task objectives, deadlines, and expected outcomes clearly.

4. **Monitor and Support:** Provide guidance as needed but avoid micromanagement. Schedule a follow-up to review progress and address any challenges.

Example:

- *Task:* Preparing the monthly report.

- *Team Member:* Choose a junior team member looking to develop his/her analytical and reporting skills.

- *Expectations:* The report should cover key metrics, be error-free, and be ready by the third Friday of each month.

- *Support:* Provide access to templates and data sources, and schedule an initial check-in one week before the deadline.

QUIZ FOR PART II

Indicate whether the following statements are true (T) or false (F).

1. Communication, by its very nature, is always effective.   T   F

2. In communication, supervisors should try to sound sophisticated by using big words.   T   F

3. In communication, feedback is the medium used to deliver the message.   T   F

4. Unclear expectations lead to confusion and reduced motivation.   T   F

5. SMART goals provide a structured approach to achieving objectives.   T   F

6. The two-minute rule says, "Take two minutes before and after each task to reflect.   T   F

7. Time blocking is a colossal waste of time.   T   F

8. Supervisors should not delegate tasks that they can perform.   T   F

9. Supervisors resist the urge to adjust set goals.   T   F

10. Communication is all about talking.   T   F

ANSWERS

1 F   2 F   3 F   4 T   5 T   6 F   7 F   8 F
9 F   10 F

PART III
BUILDING AND LEADING
HIGH-PERFORMANCE
TEAMS

CHAPTER 7
MOTIVATING AND
ENGAGING YOUR TEAM

Chapter Overview

The task of motivating and engaging your team is essential to unlocking team members' full potential and fostering a productive, positive workplace. An engaged team is more likely to stay committed, work harder, and produce high-quality results. In this chapter, we will explore methods to encourage motivation, address factors influencing engagement, and create an environment where every team member feels valued.

Key Learning Objectives

By the end of this chapter, you should be able to:

1. Understand the role of motivation in team dynamics and performance.

2. Identify common motivators and de-motivators in the workplace.

3. Develop techniques to engage team members based on their individual needs and preferences.

4. Apply strategies to foster a supportive and empowering work environment.

5. Measure and maintain team engagement for sustained performance.

Section 1:
Understanding the Power of Motivation

Motivation is a driving force that determines how much effort team members are willing to put into their work. Supervisors who understand what motivates their teams can create an environment where individuals are more likely to excel and reach their goals.

Practical Steps

Identify Intrinsic vs. Extrinsic Motivation

Intrinsic motivation comes from within—such as personal satisfaction or a sense of achievement. Extrinsic motivation, on the other hand, comes from external rewards like bonuses or recognition. Understanding these distinctions helps you apply the right motivators for each team member. The following table shows a list of intrinsic and extrinsic motivators.

Table 7.1 Intrinsic and Extrinsic Motivators

Intrinsic Motivators	Extrinsic Motivators
1. **Personal Growth:** The desire to learn new skills, develop expertise, or pursue self-improvement.	1. **Financial Incentives:** Bonuses, salary increases, or other financial rewards linked to performance.
2. **Sense of Accomplishment:** The satisfaction and pride that comes from achieving challenging goals or completing tasks.	2. **Public Recognition:** Awards, certificates, or "Employee of the Month" acknowledgments that highlight accomplishments.
3. **Passion for the Work:** Genuine interest and enthusiasm for the job or task itself, regardless of external rewards.	3. **Promotions and Career Advancement:** Opportunities for higher positions, more responsibility, or increased status within the organization.
4. **Autonomy:** The enjoyment of having control over one's work and making independent decisions.	4. **Job Security:** Reassurance or incentives that strengthen one's position in the organization, reducing concerns about job loss.

Recognize Unique Motivators

Each team member has unique drivers. Some may value personal growth, while others prioritize financial incentives or job security. Engage in one-on-one conversations to understand what truly motivates each individual.

Section 2: Addressing Common De-Motivators in the Workplace

Understanding and mitigating de-motivators can help maintain a high level of team morale. Common de-motivators include lack of recognition, unclear goals, poor communication, and excessive stress.

Practical Steps

Recognize and Address Burnout

Heavy workloads or unclear expectations can quickly lead to burnout. Make it a priority to monitor stress levels and adjust workloads as needed.

Promote Fairness and Transparency

Favoritism or unclear performance metrics can lead to dissatisfaction. Establish clear, fair processes for evaluations and reward distribution.

Encourage Open Communication

Make it easy for team members to express concerns or challenges they face. An approachable supervisor who listens actively can help alleviate stress and solve problems early on.

Section 3: Engaging Team Members by Fostering a Sense of Purpose

People are more engaged when they feel that their work has meaning. Helping team members see the larger impact of their contributions can increase their sense of purpose and commitment.

Practical Steps

Connect Individual Goals to Organizational Objectives

Show team members how their work aligns with the company's mission and goals. Knowing that their efforts contribute to a greater purpose boosts motivation.

Celebrate Milestones and Achievements

Recognize the completion of significant projects or milestones, even small ones. Publicly celebrating achievements enhances the sense of purpose and boosts morale.

Encourage Professional Development

Offer training, mentorship, or other growth opportunities to help team members develop skills and advance their careers.

Section 4: Creating a Culture of Recognition and Appreciation

Recognition is one of the most effective ways to enhance motivation and engagement. Regular, genuine appreciation for contributions reinforces positive behavior and makes team members feel valued.

Practical Steps

Implement a Recognition Program

Formal recognition programs, such as "Employee of the Month," can provide structure to your appreciation efforts. Ensure the program is inclusive and based on objective criteria.

Provide Real-Time Feedback

Don't wait for annual reviews to offer feedback. Positive reinforcement given in real time has a powerful impact and encourages continued strong performance.

Celebrate Efforts, Not Just Outcomes

Recognize the hard work that team members put in, even if the results aren't perfect. Showing appreciation for their effort can encourage them to keep improving and trying new things.

Section 5: Enhancing Engagement Through Autonomy and Trust

Autonomy is a powerful motivator. Supervisors who give team members more control over their work and decision-making processes foster greater engagement and creativity.

Practical Steps

Delegate Meaningful Tasks

Assign tasks that challenge team members and allow them to make decisions. Avoid micromanagement and trust your team to meet expectations.

Encourage Innovative Thinking

Give team members the freedom to explore new ideas or propose solutions. Showing that you value their input strengthens their commitment to the team's success.

Provide Opportunities for Leadership:

Offering leadership roles in projects or initiatives allows team members to build confidence and take ownership of their work.

Section 6: Maintaining High Levels of Engagement Over Time

Engagement can fluctuate due to changes in work dynamics, personal circumstances, or organizational changes. By actively managing engagement, supervisors can sustain high levels of motivation over the long term.

Practical Steps

Conduct Regular Engagement Check-Ins

Regular one-on-one meetings or team surveys provide insights into how engaged your team is and help you address issues early.

Adapt to Changing Needs

As team members' personal and professional circumstances evolve, so do their motivators. Stay flexible and responsive to their changing needs.

Encourage Work-Life Balance

Encourage healthy boundaries between work and personal life. Offering flexible work options, when possible, helps team members feel supported and prevents burnout. Supervisors play a critical role in promoting work-life balance within their teams, as it directly influences motivation and engagement. When employees feel supported in balancing professional and personal responsibilities, they are more likely to be satisfied, productive, and committed to their work. Supervisors can foster this balance by setting realistic expectations, encouraging breaks, and respecting boundaries. Leading by example—showing that it's possible to excel at work while valuing personal time—creates a culture where employees feel valued, energized, and motivated to contribute their best efforts. The accompanying diagram illustrates the concept of balance, where "Work" and "Life" are weighted on a scale, emphasizing the importance of equilibrium.

Figure 7.1 Work-life Balance

Reflection Questions

1. What are the primary motivators for each of your team members, and how can you tailor your approach to support them?

2. How often do you show appreciation for your team's hard work? Are there ways to increase your efforts in recognizing their contributions?

3. Are there any de-motivators in your team's environment that you could address to improve morale and engagement?

4. How much autonomy do your team members have in their work, and could it be increased in a way that benefits both the team and the organization?

Key Takeaways

- **Motivation and engagement** are crucial for fostering a high-performing and satisfied team.

- **Individual motivators vary**, and understanding them is key to a tailored supervisory approach.

- **Recognition and appreciation** are powerful motivators that create a positive and committed team culture.

- **Autonomy and trust** build a stronger, more engaged team, encouraging innovation and ownership.

- **Regular check-ins** help supervisors stay informed about team morale and address engagement challenges promptly.

Practical Application Exercise

Design a Recognition Strategy

1. **Identify Key Areas for Recognition:** List specific achievements or behaviors you would like to recognize, such as project completion, innovative thinking, or teamwork.

2. **Choose the Method of Recognition:** Decide whether you'll recognize team members publicly (e.g., in team meetings) or privately (e.g., with personalized notes).

3. **Implement and Monitor:** Put your recognition strategy into practice. Observe its impact on team morale and engagement, and adjust as needed.

Example

- *Recognize:* Outstanding teamwork and problem-solving.

- *Method:* Verbal recognition during weekly team meetings and an occasional "thank-you" email highlighting specific contributions.

- *Monitor:* Observe engagement levels and ask for team feedback to ensure the strategy is meaningful.

CHAPTER 8
PERFORMANCE MANAGEMENT AND FEEDBACK

Chapter Overview

Performance management and feedback are essential tools for any supervisor striving to build a high-performing team. When implemented effectively, these processes not only enhance individual and team performance but also foster motivation, alignment with organizational goals, and a culture of continuous improvement. This chapter is organized to guide supervisors through the key components of performance management, providing practical strategies and examples.

Key Learning Objectives

By the end of this chapter, you should be able to:

1. Understand the role and benefits of performance management in a supervisory position.

2. Set clear, measurable performance expectations for team members.

3. Conduct ongoing performance reviews and manage performance progress.

4. Deliver constructive feedback that motivates improvement.

5. Recognize and reward achievements in a meaningful way.

Section 1: The Importance of Performance Management

Effective performance management is the cornerstone of successful teams. Supervisors play a critical role in fostering an environment where employees are clear about their goals, receive support to meet these goals, and are recognized for their accomplishments. When performance management is done well, it not only boosts team morale but also increases organizational productivity and employee retention.

Key Points

Performance management:

- Drives alignment between individual contributions and organizational goals.

- Encourages personal and professional growth within the team.

- Reduces misunderstandings and conflicts by establishing clear expectations.

Section 2:
Setting Performance Expectations

To effectively manage performance, supervisors must set clear and measurable expectations that team members can understand and work toward.

Practical Steps

Define Roles and Responsibilities: Make sure team members know what's expected of them in their roles.

Use SMART Goals: Goals should be Specific, Measurable, Achievable, Relevant, and Time-bound to provide clear direction.

Create Alignment with Organizational Objectives: Show how each role contributes to larger company goals.

Section 3: Managing Performance Progress

Supervisors should keep track of each team member's progress toward his/her goals, providing guidance, support, and feedback along the way.

Practical Steps

Regular Check-Ins: Conduct periodic one-on-one meetings to review progress, address challenges, and offer guidance.

Encourage Self-Reflection: Help team members assess their own performance and identify areas for improvement.

Document Progress: Keep a record of meetings, feedback, and progress to support future reviews and decision-making.

Section 4:
Delivering Constructive Feedback

Constructive feedback is essential for reinforcing positive behaviors and addressing areas for improvement. When delivered effectively, it can inspire growth and improvement.

Feedback Techniques

Be Timely: Give feedback soon after the observed behavior to make it relevant and actionable.

Focus on Behaviors, Not Traits: Address specific actions rather than personality traits to keep feedback objective and constructive.

Use the Feedback Sandwich: Begin with a positive observation, address areas for improvement, and end with encouragement. The following diagram illustrates the feedback sandwich.

Figure 8.1 The Feedback Sandwich

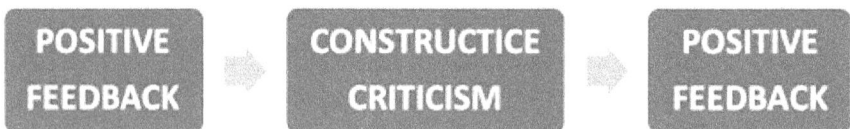

Section 5:
Recognizing and Rewarding Success

Recognition and rewards are powerful tools for motivation, helping team members feel valued and appreciated. When employees see that their hard work is recognized, they are more likely to stay engaged and motivated.

Practical Steps

Tailor Recognition to the Individual: Use rewards that are meaningful to the specific team member, whether it's public praise, a note of appreciation, or a tangible reward.

Celebrate Both Individual and Team Achievements: Balance individual recognition with team-based celebrations to foster collaboration and unity.

Encourage Peer Recognition: Allow team members to recognize each other's contributions, creating a culture of appreciation within the team.

Section 6: Addressing Underperformance

Handling underperformance is one of the most challenging aspects of supervision, but it is crucial for maintaining team morale and productivity. Supervisors must address underperformance in a supportive yet structured way.

Practical Steps

Identify the Cause: Determine whether the underperformance is due to skill gaps, personal issues, lack of clarity, or motivation.

Develop a Performance Improvement Plan (PIP): Outline clear goals, timelines, and resources to support improvement.

Provide Ongoing Support: Offer guidance and resources as needed, and check in regularly to monitor progress.

Reflection Questions

1. How can I ensure that my feedback is motivating rather than discouraging?

2. What are some ways to make goal-setting a collaborative process with my team?

3. How can I balance recognition between high achievers and other team members to maintain fairness?

4. What strategies can I use to address underperformance while keeping morale intact?

Key Takeaways

- **Clear Expectations Set the Stage for Success:** Defining roles and SMART goals ensures that team members know what's expected.

- **Continuous Feedback Drives Improvement:** Regular feedback helps team members adjust and grow.

- **Recognition Reinforces Positive Behavior:** Celebrating success encourages motivation and loyalty.

- **Addressing Underperformance is Key:** Supportive intervention prevents issues from escalating and helps team members reach their potential.

Practical Application Exercise

Think of a recent situation with a team member who either excelled or struggled. Using the concepts from this chapter:

1. **Identify the behavior** and determine the most appropriate feedback approach.

2. **Prepare a brief feedback conversation** using the Feedback Sandwich method.

3. **Consider a recognition or improvement plan**, based on whether the behavior was positive or needs adjustment.

Example: Performance Management and Feedback Scenario

Scenario:

Maria, a team member, has consistently met her deadlines but sometimes rushes through details, leading to minor mistakes.

Approach:

1. **Begin with praise:** "Maria, your dedication to meeting deadlines is truly impressive, and I appreciate your commitment."

2. **Address areas for improvement:** "One area we could work on is attention to detail. Taking a bit

more time to review your work could prevent small errors."

3. **End positively:** "I'm confident that with a little extra focus, your contributions will have an even greater impact. Let me know if there's anything I can do to support you in this."

This approach combines recognition with constructive feedback, encouraging Maria to continue her strengths while focusing on improvement areas.

By following these performance management and feedback techniques, supervisors can create a team environment where team member feel supported, valued, and motivated to reach their full potential. In the next chapter, **Conflict Resolution and Problem-Solving**, we'll explore strategies to address and resolve conflicts within the team, ensuring a harmonious and productive workplace.

CHAPTER 9
CONFLICT RESOLUTION
AND PROBLEM-SOLVING

Chapter Overview

Conflict is a natural part of any workplace, arising from diverse perspectives, goals, and personalities. How a supervisor manages conflict and approaches problem-solving significantly affects team morale, productivity, and cohesion. This chapter focuses on strategies to address conflict constructively and turn potential challenges into opportunities for growth and collaboration.

Key Learning Objectives

By the end of this chapter, you should be able to:

1. Recognize the sources and types of conflicts that commonly arise in teams.

2. Understand different conflict resolution styles and their appropriate uses.

3. Apply effective problem-solving techniques to resolve conflicts.

4. Encourage open communication to prevent and manage disagreements.

5. Create an action plan for fostering a collaborative team environment.

Section 1:
Understanding the Nature of Conflict

Conflicts arise from various sources, including misunderstandings, competing goals, and differences in values or working styles. Supervisors who recognize the nature and root causes of conflicts are better equipped to address them constructively.

Common Causes of Conflict

Communication Issues: Misunderstandings due to unclear or incomplete information.

Resource Allocation: Competition for limited resources, such as time, budget, or materials.

Personality Clashes: Differences in personalities and working styles.

Role Ambiguity: Confusion over roles and responsibilities.

Competing Goals: Conflicts between personal, team, or organizational objectives.

Section 2: Conflict Resolution Styles

There is no one-size-fits-all solution to managing conflicts. The most effective supervisors understand various conflict resolution styles and select the one most appropriate for the situation.

Five Conflict Resolution Styles

1. Avoiding: Withdrawing from the conflict. Useful for minor issues or when emotions are high, but can lead to unresolved issues.

2. Accommodating: Putting others' needs first. Effective for minor conflicts or when a quick resolution is needed but can lead to resentment if overused.

3. Competing: Assertively pursuing one's own interests. Useful for urgent matters but may damage relationships if overused.

4. Compromising: Finding a middle ground. Good for balancing interests but may result in neither party feeling fully satisfied.

5. Collaborating: Working together to find a win-win solution. The most constructive approach but requires time and effort.

Section 3: Steps for Conflict Resolution

When faced with a conflict, following a clear, step-by-step approach can help supervisors manage the situation effectively and maintain team harmony.

Practical Steps:

1. **Acknowledge the Conflict:** Address the issue early to prevent escalation.

2. **Listen Actively:** Allow each party to share their perspective without interruption.

3. **Identify the Root Cause:** Focus on the underlying issue rather than surface-level disagreements.

4. **Brainstorm Solutions:** Encourage all parties to contribute possible resolutions.

5. **Agree on a Solution:** Collaborate on a mutually agreeable solution that addresses the root cause.

6. **Follow-Up:** Check in after a resolution to ensure the conflict is fully resolved and no lingering issues remain.

The conflict resolution process is illustrated in the following diagram.

Figure 9.1 The Conflict Resolution Process

Section 4: Problem-Solving Techniques for Supervisors

Supervisors frequently encounter problems that require quick thinking and practical solutions. Problem-solving techniques are essential tools for turning obstacles into opportunities. Here are some techniques for effective problem-solving.

Techniques for Effective Problem-Solving

Define the Problem Clearly: Break down the problem into specific issues to tackle them more effectively.

Analyze Possible Causes: Use tools like the "5 Whys" technique to identify root causes. An example of the use of the "5 Whys" technique is shown in the table below. The current problem is that a team missed a project deadline.

Brainstorm Solutions: Generate multiple solutions to find the most effective and feasible one.

Evaluate and Decide: Assess potential solutions based on criteria such as time, cost, and impact.

Implement and Review: Put the solution into action and review its effectiveness to learn from the outcome.

Table 9.1 An Illustration of the Use of the 5 Whys Techniques

Question	Answer
1. Why was the deadline missed?	The tasks took longer than expected
2. Why did the tasks take longer?	The team encountered unexpected technical issues
3. Why were these issues not expected?	The project requirements were not fully clarified at the outset
4. Why weren't the requirements fully clarified?	The team didn't hold a detailed planning session with the client
5. Why wasn't there a detailed planning session?	There was no standard procedure for initiating a planning session before starting a project.

Root Cause: A lack of a standard project planning procedure led to unclear requirements, which ultimately delayed the project.

Section 5: Fostering a Culture of Open Communication

Encouraging a culture where team members feel safe expressing their views and resolving issues respectfully can prevent conflicts from arising in the first place.

Practical Steps

Set Clear Communication Norms: Establish guidelines for respectful, open communication.

Encourage Transparency: Be open about challenges and solicit feedback from the team.

Provide a Safe Space for Feedback: Make it easy for team members to voice concerns without fear of retribution.

Model Open Communication: Show vulnerability and openness as a leader to encourage the same in others.

Reflection Questions

1. Which conflict resolution style do I most commonly use, and is it always the most effective?

2. How can I foster an environment where team members feel comfortable bringing conflicts to my attention?

3. What steps can I take to improve my active listening skills during conflict situations?

4. How can I balance assertiveness with empathy when addressing conflicts?

Key Takeaways

- **Conflict is Inevitable:** Understanding the causes of conflict can help prevent misunderstandings and address issues early.

- **Conflict Styles Vary:** Choose a conflict resolution style appropriate to the situation to maintain healthy team relationships.

- **Problem-solving techniques are Essential:** Structured problem-solving ensures that solutions address the root cause, not just the symptoms.

- **Open Communication Reduces Conflict:** Supervisors who foster a culture of open communication often see fewer conflicts and quicker resolutions.

Practical Application Exercise

Reflect on a recent conflict or problem within your team. Using the concepts from this chapter:

1. **Identify the conflict resolution style** you used (or wish you had used).

2. **Outline the steps you took** (or would take) to address the issue, following the conflict resolution steps in this chapter.

3. **Consider how fostering open communication** could help prevent similar conflicts in the future.

Example: Conflict Resolution Scenario

Scenario: Two team members, Alex and Jamie, have differing approaches to a project deadline. Alex wants to focus on quality, while Jamie prioritizes meeting the deadline.

Approach:

1. **Acknowledge the conflict:** Hold a meeting to openly discuss the disagreement.

2. **Listen actively:** Allow both Alex and Jamie to explain their viewpoints without interruptions.

3. **Identify the root cause:** Recognize that the issue stems from conflicting priorities of quality versus timeliness.

4. **Brainstorm solutions:** Encourage Alex and Jamie to suggest ways to balance quality and deadline constraints.

5. **Agree on a solution:** Decide to allocate extra resources to ensure both goals are met.

6. **Follow up:** Check in with Alex and Jamie later to ensure they feel satisfied with the compromise.

This approach not only resolves the immediate conflict but also reinforces the value of collaboration and compromise within the team.

By implementing the conflict resolution and problem-solving strategies outlined in this chapter, supervisors can manage conflicts constructively, maintain team harmony, and foster an environment of trust and collaboration. In the next chapter, **Chapter 10: Navigating Change and Managing Transitions**, we'll explore ways whereby supervisors can lead their teams through change.

QUIZ FOR PART III

Indicate whether the following statements are true (T) or false (F).

1. People are very much alike so they are motivated by the same factors. T   F

2. It is well known that salary increases will motivate all workers.   T   F

3. Job security is an extrinsic motivator.   T   F

4. Work-life balance is a method of estimating the monetary value of life.   T   F

5. Performance management boosts morale.   T   F

6. The feedback sandwich is fed to poor team members.   T   F

7. Recognition reinforces behavior. T   F

8. As long as there is a common goal, conflict cannot arise. T   F

9. The "5 Whys" technique helps to identify root causes of problems.   T   F

10. Conflict can be reduced by open communication.   T   F

ANSWERS

1 F   2 F   3 T   4 F   5 T   6 F   7 T   8 F
9 T   10 T

PART IV
ADVANCED
SUPERVISORY
PRACTICES

CHAPTER 10
NAVIGATING CHANGE AND MANAGING TRANSITIONS

Chapter Overview

Change is inevitable in any organization, and effective supervisors must be equipped to lead their teams through these periods of transition with confidence and clarity. This chapter delves into understanding the nature of organizational change, identifying and managing the stages of change, communicating effectively during transitions, and supporting team members as they adjust. We also cover techniques for maintaining productivity and morale, even in uncertain times and fostering a resilient, adaptable team culture.

Key Learning Objectives

By the end of this chapter, you should be able to:

1. Identify the different types of organizational change and their impact on teams.

2. Understand the psychological stages of change and how individuals typically respond to transitions.

3. Develop effective communication strategies to reduce uncertainty and build trust during change.

4. Use practical techniques to help team members adapt and remain productive.

5. Cultivate a resilient team mindset to face future challenges with confidence.

Section 1:
Understanding Organizational Change

Organizational change can take many forms, each with distinct implications for teams and individual roles. Common types of change include:

Structural Change: Adjustments in organizational hierarchy, such as mergers, acquisitions, or departmental restructuring. These often lead to shifts in reporting lines, team dynamics, and job responsibilities, potentially causing confusion and stress.

Strategic Change: Changes in the organization's direction or priorities, such as a new business model, product lines, or market expansion. Such shifts can affect team objectives and require a re-evaluation of goals.

Technological Change: Adopting new systems, software, or equipment. Technological changes can improve efficiency but may require upskilling or retraining, affecting productivity as team members adapt.

Cultural Change: Shifts in organizational values, norms, or workplace policies. Cultural change often requires supervisors to model new behaviors and facilitate open discussions about adapting to a new environment.

Understanding these categories helps supervisors anticipate the challenges each type of change presents, positioning them to better support their teams.

Section 2: The Stages of Change

The psychological process individuals undergo during change is often referred to as the "Change Curve," which typically involves the following stages:

1. **Denial:** Initial resistance or disbelief about the need for change. Team members may ignore the change or downplay its significance.

2. **Resistance:** As the reality of the change sets in, some individuals experience frustration, anxiety, or anger. This stage often includes pushback as team members cling to familiar routines.

3. **Exploration:** In this stage, individuals begin to accept the change and explore new ways of working. Creativity and openness to new ideas emerge as individuals adapt.

4. **Commitment:** Finally, team members embrace the change and integrate it into their work routines. Productivity increases, and morale stabilizes as the team moves forward.

The four stages of change can be illustrated by the following diagram.

By recognizing these stages, supervisors can tailor their approach to each team member's unique position on the Change Curve, offering targeted support and interventions.

Figure 10.1 The Four Stages of Change

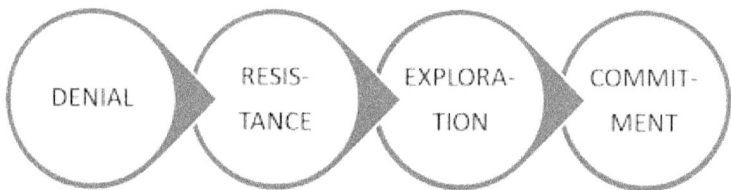

Section 3:
Communicating During Transitions

Effective communication is essential in managing change. Supervisors should aim to:

Set Clear Expectations

From the outset, explain why the change is happening, how it aligns with organizational goals, and what team members can expect in terms of timelines, roles, and responsibilities.

Provide Regular Updates

Maintaining an open line of communication throughout the transition period is crucial. Schedule regular check-ins and send updates, even if the only update is that there are no new developments.

Empathize with Concerns

Acknowledge the emotions and concerns your team may have. Open the floor for questions, encourage feedback, and address anxieties to reduce fear and resistance.

Adapt Your Message

Tailor your messaging based on individual responses. Some may appreciate detailed information, while others prefer high-level overviews. Adjust your approach to suit each team member's communication style.

Highlight Positive Outcomes

Reinforce the benefits of the change and its potential positive impact on the team's work or the organization's success. Focus on creating a shared sense of purpose around the change.

Section 4: Supporting Team Adaptation

To help your team adapt successfully to change, consider implementing these supportive strategies:

Promote Flexibility

Encourage team members to approach new tasks or roles with an open mind. Recognize that adjusting to change takes time and allow for flexibility in deadlines and expectations as team members adapt.

Provide Training and Resources

Offer any necessary upskilling or training sessions to ease the transition, especially if the change involves new technology or processes. Accessible resources help team members feel equipped to succeed.

Acknowledge Individual Contributions

Recognize and celebrate team members who demonstrate adaptability, resilience, and a positive attitude toward the change. Acknowledgment reinforces desired behaviors and encourages others to embrace the shift.

Build a Support Network

Create opportunities for peer support and team-building activities. By fostering connections, team members can share experiences and coping strategies, reducing feelings of isolation.

Section 5:
Maintaining Productivity and Morale

Productivity and morale are often affected by change, and supervisors need strategies to manage both. Consider the following:

Set Short-Term Goals

During transitions, long-term goals may feel overwhelming. Break objectives into achievable milestones to maintain momentum and give team members a sense of progress.

Celebrate Small Wins

Recognize achievements, no matter how small, as the team adjusts. Celebrations encourage motivation and reinforce the idea that progress is happening.

Maintain Transparency

When team members feel informed, they are more likely to trust leadership and remain engaged. Be honest about challenges or setbacks while emphasizing your team's resilience and potential.

Foster a Growth Mindset

Encourage team members to view challenges as opportunities for growth. Reinforcing a growth mindset during change can increase resilience and empower your team to tackle future transitions with confidence.

Reflection Questions

1. How have you handled change in the past, and what did you learn from those experiences?

2. What steps can you take to improve your communication style when leading a team through change?

3. How can you make change feel less overwhelming for your team members?

Key Takeaways

- **Understand the Nature of Change:** Each type of change requires a unique approach, from setting expectations to offering support.

- **Address Emotions:** Acknowledge and address the psychological impact of change on team members.

- **Communicate Effectively:** Consistent, empathetic communication helps reduce resistance and fosters trust.

- **Support Adaptation:** By offering training, promoting flexibility, and building a support network, supervisors can help teams adjust.

- **Boost Morale:** Use short-term goals and celebrate successes to sustain morale and engagement.

Practical Application Exercise

Scenario: Your organization is undergoing a transition to a new project management software. Some team members are apprehensive about the learning curve, while others are concerned it may disrupt their workflows.

Instructions:

1. **Draft a Communication Plan:** Write a plan to introduce the new software, including key talking points for the initial announcement, anticipated questions, and strategies for managing resistance.

2. **Outline a Training Program:** Design a brief outline for training sessions that provide essential skills, tips, and resources for using the software efficiently.

3. **Create a Support Schedule:** Develop a schedule of follow-up meetings or check-ins where team members can discuss challenges and provide feedback on their experiences.

Example

Scenario: Jordan, a supervisor, was informed that her department would be moving to a new performance review system. She anticipated that some team members might resist the change, so she took a proactive approach.

Actions Taken:

1. **Prepared and Communicated Clearly:** Jordan held a meeting to introduce the new system, explaining its benefits and addressing common concerns upfront.

2. **Organized Hands-On Training:** She arranged for a series of training sessions, allowing team members to practice with the new system and ask questions in a supportive environment.

3. **Followed Up Consistently:** Jordan held weekly check-ins to discuss any ongoing challenges. She acknowledged team members' adaptability and celebrated small milestones as they became comfortable with the system.

Through her proactive planning, Jordan successfully helped her team embrace the new system, keeping morale high and promoting a positive attitude toward change.

Navigating change is a vital skill for supervisors. By mastering these techniques, you can lead your team through transitions with empathy, clarity, and resilience, fostering an adaptable and united team culture.

CHAPTER 11
COACHING AND DEVELOPING TEAM MEMBERS

Chapter Overview

Supervisors play a pivotal role in fostering growth and development within their teams. Effective coaching and development strategies not only enhance individual performance but also contribute to team success and organizational goals. This chapter explores the fundamentals of coaching, the importance of development plans, and how to cultivate a culture of continuous learning and improvement.

Key Learning Objectives

By the end of this chapter, you should be able to:

1. Understand the role of coaching in team development.

2. Differentiate between coaching, mentoring, and training.

3. Create personalized development plans for team members.

4. Implement feedback strategies to guide and inspire growth.

5. Foster a learning environment that encourages self-improvement and skill-building.

Section 1: The Role of Coaching in Team Development

Coaching is a cornerstone of effective supervision. Unlike mentoring or training, coaching focuses on helping employees unlock their potential through guidance and active problem-solving.

Key Components of Effective Coaching

Active Listening: Fully understanding the employee's perspective.

Goal Alignment: Ensuring individual goals align with team and organizational objectives.

Supportive Feedback: Offering constructive and motivational input to encourage growth.

The Benefits of Coaching

Organizations enjoy the following benefits of coaching:

- Improved employee performance and confidence.
- Strengthened relationships between supervisors and employees.
- Enhanced problem-solving and critical thinking skills within the team.

Section 2: Crafting Personalized Development Plans

A well-designed development plan serves as a roadmap for growth, tailored to each team member's unique needs and aspirations.

Steps to Create Effective Development Plans

In creating an effective development plan, it is wise to follow these steps.

1. **Assessment:** Evaluate the employee's current skills and potential.

2. **Goal Setting:** Define SMART (Specific, Measurable, Achievable, Relevant, Time-bound) objectives.

3. **Resource Allocation:** Identify the tools, training, and support needed.

4. **Milestone Setting:** Break the plan into manageable phases.

5. **Review and Adjust:** Monitor progress and refine the plan as needed.

Figure 11.1 Steps for Creating Development Plan

Section 3: Providing Feedback for Growth

Feedback is a powerful tool when delivered constructively. It helps employees understand their performance and provides a clear path to improvement.

Techniques for Effective Feedback

You may find the following feedback techniques helpful:

- **The Sandwich Approach:** Start with a positive note, address areas for improvement, and end on a motivational tone. See Chapter 8.

- **Behavioral Feedback:** Focus on specific actions rather than personal attributes.

- **Timely Delivery:** Provide feedback close to the event to ensure relevance and impact.

Common Feedback Pitfalls to Avoid

Here are a few common feedback pitfalls to avoid.

- Vagueness or lack of clarity.

- Overemphasis on negatives without offering solutions.

- Delivering feedback in public settings, which can lead to embarrassment.

You may say that this is just common sense, but we must remember Voltaire's popular saying, "Common sense is not so common."

Section 4: Fostering a Learning Culture

A culture of continuous learning empowers team members to take ownership of their growth.

Strategies to Promote Learning

As a supervisor, you can promote learning by employing the following strategies:

- **Encourage Self-Development:** Provide resources for independent learning, such as books, online courses, or workshops.
- **Celebrate Growth:** Acknowledge and reward progress to motivate ongoing effort.
- **Lead by Example:** Demonstrate your commitment to learning through your actions.

Reflection Questions

1. What challenges have you faced when coaching team members, and how did you address them?

2. How do you currently track and measure employee development progress?

3. What steps can you take to create a stronger learning culture within your team?

Key Takeaways

- Coaching is an interactive process that helps employees unlock their potential and achieve their goals.
- Personalized development plans are essential for fostering employee growth and aligning efforts with organizational objectives.

- Constructive feedback delivered with care and precision can inspire improvement and strengthen trust.

- A learning culture encourages innovation, resilience, and continuous improvement within the team.

Practical Application Exercise

1. **Case Study:** Identify a team member who could benefit from coaching. Create a development plan for this individual, including specific goals, milestones, and resources.

2. **Role-Playing Feedback:** Practice delivering constructive feedback using the sandwich approach with a colleague or peer.

Example: Coaching in Action

Sarah, a new sales associate, struggled to meet her monthly targets. Her supervisor, Tim, initiated a coaching session to understand her challenges. After listening actively, Tim discovered Sarah lacked confidence in handling objections. Together, they created a development plan focusing on objection-handling techniques, role-playing exercises, and weekly check-ins. Over three months, Sarah's confidence grew, and she began exceeding her targets. This success story highlights how personalized coaching can drive performance and morale.

By implementing these coaching and development strategies, you can empower your team members to achieve their potential and contribute meaningfully to organizational success.

CHAPTER 12
BUILDING ACCOUNTABILITY AND OWNERSHIP

Chapter Overview

Accountability and ownership are essential elements of a high-performing team. When team members take responsibility for their actions and embrace their roles with commitment, they foster trust, collaboration, and productivity. In this chapter, we explore strategies to cultivate accountability and ownership, the role of supervisors in modeling these behaviors, and practical tools to reinforce these principles within a team.

Key Learning Objectives

By the end of this chapter, you should be able to:

1. Understand the importance of accountability and ownership in team dynamics.

2. Identify obstacles that hinder accountability and strategies to overcome them.

3. Implement systems and practices that encourage team members to take responsibility.

4. Model accountability as a leader to inspire similar behavior in others.

5. Foster a team culture where ownership is celebrated and rewarded.

Section 1: The Importance of Accountability and Ownership

Accountability ensures that team members fulfill their commitments and take responsibility for their actions. Ownership, on the other hand, reflects an individual's emotional investment in his/her work. Together, these attributes:

- Build trust within the team.

- Enhance efficiency and productivity.

- Minimize finger-pointing and blame-shifting during challenges.

- Encourage proactive problem-solving.

The Ripple Effect of Accountability

When accountability is established at all levels, it cascades through the team, creating a culture where everyone feels empowered and motivated to deliver his/her best.

Section 2: Overcoming Barriers to Accountability

Despite its importance, accountability can be challenging to establish. Common barriers include:

Ambiguity in Roles: Unclear expectations lead to confusion and inaction.

Fear of Failure: Employees may avoid taking responsibility to shield themselves from criticism.

Lack of Feedback: Without constructive feedback, employees may not understand their performance gaps.

Poor Communication: Miscommunication can derail efforts to uphold accountability.

Strategies to Address Barriers

The following are strategies that supervisors can use to overcome barriers to accountability:

- Clearly define roles, responsibilities, and expectations.

- Foster a supportive environment where mistakes are viewed as learning opportunities.

- Provide timely, specific feedback to guide improvement.

- Maintain open channels of communication to minimize misunderstandings.

Section 3: Practical Strategies for Building Accountability

How does a supervisor build accountability? Well, there are a few strategies in the supervisor's toolkit. They include:

1. Set Clear Expectations

- Clearly articulate goals, deadlines, and deliverables.
- Use SMART (Specific, Measurable, Achievable, Realistic, Time-bound) criteria to define expectations.

2. Encourage Personal Responsibility

- Assign tasks based on individual strengths and interests.
- Allow employees to take ownership of projects from start to finish.

3. Monitor Progress Without Micromanaging

- Schedule regular check-ins to review progress.
- Provide autonomy while remaining available for guidance.

4. Reward Accountability

- Recognize and celebrate team members who demonstrate accountability.
- Offer incentives for meeting and exceeding goals.

These strategies for building accountability are illustrated in Figure 12.1 below.

Figure 12.1 Strategies for Building Accountability

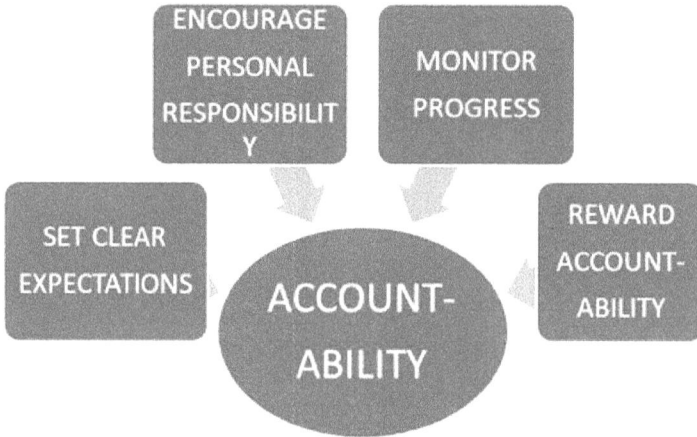

Section 4: The Supervisor's Role in Modeling Accountability

Supervisors play an important role in modeling accountability. They set the tone for accountability within the team. To lead by example:

Own Your Decisions: Accept responsibility for outcomes, both positive and negative.

Deliver on Commitments: Meet deadlines and follow through on promises.

Admit Mistakes: You are not infallible. Show humility and a willingness to learn from errors.

By modeling these behaviors, supervisors inspire team members to emulate them.

Reflection Questions

1. How do you currently address accountability issues in your team?

2. What changes can you make to create a culture of ownership among your team members?

3. How can you better model accountability as a supervisor?

Key Takeaways

- Accountability and ownership are crucial for team success and trust.

- Supervisors must clearly define expectations and foster a supportive environment to encourage responsibility.

- Modeling accountability as a leader inspires similar behavior within the team.

- Recognizing and rewarding accountable behavior reinforces a culture of ownership.

Practical Application Exercise

1. Scenario-Based Role Play

Create a hypothetical situation where a team member fails to meet a deadline. Role-play a conversation focusing on accountability, constructive feedback, and setting clearer expectations for the future.

2. Team Ownership Challenge

Identify a team project and delegate ownership to a team member. Monitor his/her progress, provide guidance as needed, and evaluate the outcomes together.

Example: Cultivating Accountability in a Team

Jessica, a marketing supervisor, noticed her team struggled to meet campaign deadlines. She implemented a new system where team members outlined their responsibilities in a shared accountability tracker. Jessica conducted weekly check-ins to review progress and offer support. Over time, the team became more proactive, meeting deadlines consistently and even exceeding goals. This example highlights how clear expectations and regular feedback can build accountability.

By embedding accountability and ownership into your supervisory practices, you empower your team to reach higher levels of performance and collaboration. This foundational principle will serve as a cornerstone for long-term success.

QUIZ FOR PART IV

Indicate whether the following statements are true (T) or false (F).

1. Behaving as if a change has not occurred is the resistance stage of change.   T   F

2. The best way to handle change is to give as little information as possible.   T   F

3. Celebrating successes sustains morale and engagement.   T   F

4. Effective coaching entails listening, goal alignment, and feedback.   T   F

5. A personal development plan is useless in coaching.   T   F

6. A culture of continuous learning empowers team members.   T   F

7. If a learning culture does not exist, it cannot be created.   T   F

8. Accountability involves taking responsibility for one's actions.   T   F

9. Ownership reflects an individual's emotional investment in his/her work.   T   F

10. One cannot model accountability.   T   F

ANSWERS

1 F   2 F   3 T   4 T   5 F   6 T   7 F   8 T
9 T   10 F

PART V

PRACTICAL SOLUTIONS TO COMMON SUPERVISORY CHALLENGES

CHAPTER 13
MANAGING REMOTE
AND HYBRID TEAMS

Chapter Overview

The rise of remote and hybrid work has transformed how teams operate and how supervisors lead. In this chapter, we explore strategies to effectively manage geographically dispersed teams while maintaining productivity, trust, and engagement. Supervisors will learn how to deal with challenges unique to remote and hybrid settings, leverage technology, and foster a cohesive team culture that bridges the gap between remote and in-office employees.

Key Learning Objectives

By the end of this chapter, you should be able to:

1. Understand the dynamics of remote and hybrid team management.

2. Implement strategies to build trust and engagement across diverse team setups.

3. Use technology effectively to facilitate communication, collaboration, and accountability.

4. Overcome challenges such as isolation, burnout, and uneven access to resources.

5. Cultivate an inclusive and equitable team environment for all employees.

Section 1: Understanding Remote and Hybrid Team Dynamics

Characteristics of Remote and Hybrid Teams

Remote teams operate fully online, while hybrid teams blend in-office and remote employees. For both types of teams, flexibility is a hallmark, but it requires intentional communication and coordination.

The Role of Supervisors

The role of supervisors is essentially the same whether teams are in-house, remote, or hybrid. They act as a bridge between team members and organizational goals, and they provide clarity, connection, and resources to support team success.

Section 2: Building Trust and Engagement

The Foundations of Trust

Trust is a firm belief in the truth, reliability, or ability of someone. The relationship between a supervisor and his or her team should be built on trust. Trust is built on reliability, communication, and fairness. As a supervisor, you should avoid micromanagement; instead, empower team members with autonomy.

Fostering Engagement

In addition to building trust, supervisors are responsible for keeping their teams engaged. Employee engagement refers to the extent to which employees are committed to helping their organization achieve its goals. It's demonstrated by how employees think, feel, and act, as well as the emotional connection employees feel towards their organization, their work, and their team. To foster engagement:

- Regularly check in with team members to understand their challenges and needs.

- Celebrate successes and acknowledge individual contributions, regardless of team location.

Section 3: Leveraging Technology for Success

There is no doubt that this is a technological age. This current era of human civilization is characterized by the widespread use of digital technology and the Internet. Supervisors can take advantage of available technology to lead their teams to success. Here are a few hints:

Choosing the Right Tools

Use project management software like Asana or Trello to track tasks and deadlines.

Rely on communication tools like Slack for asynchronous updates and Zoom for virtual meetings.

Enhancing Collaboration

Create shared digital workspaces to streamline document sharing and team brainstorming.

Use polls or surveys to collect feedback on the effectiveness of technology.

Section 4: Overcoming Common Challenges

Remote and hybrid teams face some challenges including, but not limited to, isolation and resource inequity. The following hints should be helpful.

1. Combating Isolation and Burnout

- Schedule informal virtual meetups to foster camaraderie.

- Promote work-life balance by encouraging breaks and flexible schedules.

2. Addressing Resource Inequities

- Provide equal access to technology, such as laptops and internet stipends.

- Ensure hybrid team members have similar opportunities for professional growth.

3. Managing Performance Across Locations

- Establish clear goals and evaluate outcomes rather than focusing on hours worked.

- Use regular one-on-one meetings to discuss progress and address roadblocks.

Section 5: Cultivating an Inclusive and Equitable Team Environment

Creating an inclusive and equitable environment for remote and hybrid teams is essential to fostering a sense of belonging, improving morale, and driving team performance. As a supervisor, your actions set the tone for fairness, respect, and mutual understanding within your team. This section outlines strategies to ensure all employees feel valued and supported, regardless of their physical work location.

Ensuring Inclusivity in Communication

To ensure inclusivity in communication, supervisors should:

Use Tools That Level the Playing Field

Incorporate technologies such as video conferencing, shared documents, and chat platforms to ensure remote employees can participate equally in discussions.

Encourage Equal Participation

During meetings, actively invite contributions from remote team members who may hesitate to speak up in virtual settings.

Create a "Digital-first" Culture

Even when some team members are in the office, use virtual platforms for meetings and collaboration to ensure no one feels excluded.

Example: A hybrid team implemented a policy where all meetings include virtual links, even for in-office staff.

They rotated facilitators, ensuring both remote and in-person employees had leadership opportunities in discussions.

Addressing Bias and Promoting Equity

Bias and inequity are likely to emerge in remote and hybrid workplaces. To address these issues, supervisors can:

Audit Work Assignments

Ensure tasks and opportunities for growth are distributed equitably across remote and in-office employees.

Avoid Proximity Bias

Proximity bias is an unintentional tendency where people in positions of power or leadership tend to favor those who are physically closer to them. It is often experienced in the workplace, where leaders may give preferential treatment to employees who work in-office at the expense of remote workers.

Do not favor in-office employees for promotions, visibility, or feedback opportunities. Regularly review performance metrics and seek input from remote team members to evaluate contributions fairly.

Champion Diversity

Celebrate cultural and geographical diversity within the team by encouraging knowledge-sharing and inclusivity-focused initiatives.

Example: A supervisor noticed that in-office employees were unintentionally given more client-facing tasks. He brought this observation to his manager. As a result, they restructured processes to assign tasks based on skills and availability rather than location, leading to more equitable distribution.

Building a Unified Team Culture

A unified team culture has certain benefits, including more effective communication, greater productivity, and better decision-making. To build a unified team culture, you can:

Foster Team Bonds

Create opportunities for team members to interact informally, such as virtual coffee breaks or hybrid team retreats.

Acknowledge Individual Contributions

Use team-wide communication channels to celebrate achievements and milestones, ensuring remote workers receive equal recognition.

Develop Shared Goals

Focus on collective goals that unite the team, emphasizing how each member's role contributes to overall success.

Example: A hybrid team supervisor organized monthly "team highlights" sessions, showcasing successes from both remote and in-office members. This boosted morale and reinforced a sense of unity.

Providing Equal Access to Resources

One way whereby you can foster an environment of inclusion and equity is by providing equal access to resources. To do so:

Standardize Tools and Support

Provide remote employees with necessary equipment, such as laptops, monitors, and ergonomic chairs, to ensure parity with in-office counterparts.

Offer Professional Development

Make training sessions, mentorship programs, and learning resources accessible to all employees. Use virtual platforms to facilitate equitable participation.

Facilitate Transparent Communication

Maintain a shared knowledge base or intranet to house important updates, policies, and project details, ensuring that remote workers are never out of the loop.

Example: A company offered remote workers a stipend to set up home offices and recorded all training sessions to ensure that time zone differences didn't prevent participation.

Measuring and Improving Inclusivity

Conduct Surveys and Feedback Sessions

Regularly solicit input from team members about their experiences and perceptions of inclusivity and equity.

Monitor Key Metrics

Track employee engagement, retention, and promotion rates across remote and in-office employees to identify and address disparities.

Take Action on Feedback

Create an action plan to address inclusivity gaps, demonstrating to your team that their voices are heard and that their opinions are valued.

Example: After receiving feedback that remote employees felt disconnected, a supervisor implemented quarterly virtual team-building exercises and established a mentorship program pairing remote and in-office staff.

Key Takeaways

- Inclusivity in remote and hybrid teams requires intentional communication, equitable resource allocation, and proactive engagement strategies.

- Supervisors must address bias, promote fairness, and ensure equal access to opportunities and recognition.

- Building a unified culture that values diversity strengthens team cohesion and morale, driving overall success.

By fostering an inclusive and equitable environment, supervisors not only enhance team satisfaction but also position their teams for long-term success in a rapidly evolving workplace landscape.

Reflection Questions

1. How can you ensure remote team members feel equally valued and engaged compared to in-office employees?

2. What steps can you take to foster trust and autonomy within your team?

3. How can technology be optimized to support your team's specific needs?

Practical Application Exercises

1. Technology Audit

- Evaluate the effectiveness of current team tools and identify areas for improvement.

- **Exercise:** List three areas where technology could better support your team. Research tools that address these gaps.

2. Team Trust-Building Activity

- Organize a virtual team-building exercise, such as sharing personal success stories or playing online collaborative games.

- **Outcome:** Strengthen interpersonal connections and trust among team members.

3. Equity Assessment

- Assess the distribution of resources and opportunities between remote and in-office employees.

- **Reflection:** Identify areas of imbalance and propose corrective actions.

Supervising remote and hybrid teams demands adaptability, empathy, and strategic planning. By implementing the strategies and tools outlined in this chapter, supervisors can overcome challenges and create a thriving, connected team environment. As workplaces continue to evolve, mastering these skills will be vital to achieving excellence in supervisory roles.

CHAPTER 14
STRESS AND CRISIS
MANAGEMENT

Chapter Overview

Every workplace faces moments of heightened stress and occasional crises. For supervisors, the ability to manage these challenges effectively can determine the morale, productivity, and overall resilience of the team. Stress and crisis management require a balance of empathy, strategic thinking, and decisive action. This chapter equips supervisors with the tools to identify stressors, implement proactive measures, and lead their teams through crises while maintaining a focus on well-being and performance.

Key Learning Objectives

By the end of this chapter, you should be able to:

1. Recognize the common causes and signs of stress within your team.

2. Employ strategies to reduce stress and foster a supportive environment.

3. Develop a structured approach to crisis management.

4. Lead your team effectively during times of uncertainty.

5. Support team members' emotional and mental well-being in stressful and crisis situations.

Section 1: Understanding Workplace Stress

Causes of Workplace Stress

Let us begin this section by answering the question: What is workplace stress? Canadian Center for Occupational Health and Safety (CCOHS) defines workplace stress as "the harmful physical and emotional responses that can happen when there is a conflict between job demands on the employee and the amount of control an employee has over meeting these demands." It continues to state that in general, the combination of high demands in a job and a low amount of control over the situation can lead to stress.

Major causes of workplace stress include:

Heavy Workloads: Unrealistic deadlines and excessive demands.

Ambiguity: Unclear roles, expectations, or lack of direction.

Interpersonal Conflicts: Difficult relationships or unresolved tensions within teams.

External Challenges: Economic instability, global events, or personal stressors.

Recognizing Signs of Stress

Supervisors may recognize the following signs of stress:

Behavioral Changes: Withdrawal, irritability, or reduced engagement.

Physical Symptoms: Fatigue, headaches, or frequent illness.

Performance Issues: Declines in productivity, quality of work, or creativity.

Team Dynamics: Increased conflicts, lack of collaboration, or overall low morale.

Example: A high-performing employee suddenly begins missing deadlines and avoids interactions. Upon addressing the issue, you discover he/she is overwhelmed by personal challenges and unclear work priorities.

Section 2: Strategies for Managing Stress

Fortunately, strategies for managing stress exist. These include the following:

Building a Resilient Team

- Foster open communication where employees feel safe sharing concerns.

- Promote work-life balance through flexible scheduling and fair workload distribution.

- Encourage teamwork and collaboration to share responsibilities.

Creating a Supportive Environment

- Provide access to wellness programs and stress-relief activities.

- Offer regular feedback and recognition to boost confidence.

- Establish clear goals and expectations to reduce ambiguity.

Practical Application

Introduce mindfulness practices during team meetings, such as guided breathing exercises, to alleviate tension and improve focus.

Section 3: Leading Through Crises

The Role of Supervisors During a Crisis

Supervisors play a major role during a crisis. They provide:

- **Leadership:** Serve as a source of stability and direction.

- **Clarity:** Communicate plans and expectations clearly.

- **Empathy:** Address the emotional needs of team members.

Developing a Crisis Management Plan

Developing a crisis management plan involves:

- **Risk Assessment:** Identify potential crises and their impact on operations.

- **Preparedness Training:** Conduct drills and establish clear protocols.

- **Role Definition:** Assign responsibilities to team members in advance.

Example: A supervisor prepared for potential IT disruptions by creating a backup communication plan and training the team in alternative workflows. When a system outage occurred, the team adapted smoothly and met critical deadlines.

Section 4: Cultivating an Inclusive and Equitable Team Environment

Why Inclusivity Matters During Stressful Times

Inclusivity matters during stressful times for the following reasons:

(a) Diverse teams bring unique perspectives to problem-solving.

(b) Inclusion fosters trust and ensures all voices are heard during crises.

Strategies for Supervisors

- Promote equitable participation in decision-making.

- Acknowledge and address disparities in how stress or crises affect team members.

- Provide tailored support, recognizing individual circumstances.

Practical Application: During a stressful project, ensure that remote and on-site employees have equal access to resources and opportunities for input.

Section 5: Supporting Emotional Well-Being

Emotional Support for Individuals

During times of stress, supervisors can:

- Be approachable for one-on-one discussions.

- Offer flexible arrangements to accommodate personal challenges.

- Encourage the use of Employee Assistance Programs (EAPs).

Team Support During Stressful Times

To support your team, as opposed to individual members, you can:

- Organize informal check-ins to build camaraderie.

- Celebrate small successes to keep morale high.

- Provide training in resilience and stress management techniques.

Example: After a high-pressure project, a supervisor organized a debriefing session and a casual team lunch to acknowledge hard work and encourage reflection.

Reflection Questions

1. What are the primary stressors affecting your team, and how can you address them?

2. How prepared is your team for a potential crisis?

3. What steps can you take to support emotional well-being in your workplace?

Key Takeaways

- Supervisors must act as both problem-solvers and emotional anchors during stressful or crisis situations.

- Proactive measures, such as open communication and team resilience-building, can mitigate the effects of stress.

- Effective crisis management emphasizes clear planning, transparent communication, and empathy.

- Supporting the emotional well-being of team members enhances overall recovery and morale.

Practical Applications and Exercises

1. Stress Audit

- **Objective:** Identify workplace stressors.

- **Activity:** Distribute an anonymous survey asking about stress sources and solutions. Use feedback to implement improvements.

2. Crisis Simulation

- **Objective:** Test the team's crisis response.

- **Activity:** Role-play a hypothetical crisis and evaluate communication, adaptability, and problem-solving skills.

3. Mindfulness Exercise

- **Objective:** Teach stress management techniques.
- **Activity:** Conduct a 10-minute guided meditation or relaxation session during a team meeting.

Stress and crises are unavoidable in today's dynamic work environments, but they are also opportunities for supervisors to demonstrate leadership and compassion. By fostering resilience, maintaining clear communication, and addressing emotional well-being, supervisors can guide their teams through challenges with confidence. Preparedness and empathy are the cornerstones of effective stress and crisis management, ensuring not only survival but growth in the face of adversity.

CHAPTER 15
DEALING WITH DIFFICULT PERSONALITIES AND SITUATIONS

Chapter Overview

Every workplace includes a diverse mix of personalities, which can be a strength but may also lead to challenging situations. Supervisors often face the task of managing difficult personalities and resolving conflicts effectively. This chapter provides practical strategies for recognizing and addressing toxic behaviors, managing challenging team dynamics, and deciding when to escalate issues to higher authorities. By mastering these skills, supervisors can maintain a healthy, productive, and collaborative work environment.

Key Learning Objectives

By the end of this chapter, you should be able to:

1. Identify toxic behaviors and their impact on team dynamics.

2. Implement strategies to address and mitigate the effects of difficult personalities.

3. Handle challenging situations with professionalism and fairness.

4. Determine when and how to escalate issues for resolution.

5. Foster a culture of respect, collaboration, and accountability.

Section 1: Recognizing and Handling Toxic Behaviors

Toxic workplace behaviors are unhealthy behaviors and attitudes that can have a detrimental effect on employees' physical, mental, and emotional health, as well as their job performance.

Common Types of Toxic Behaviors

There are many types of people who exhibit behaviors that are considered toxic. They include:

- *The Bully:* Intimidates others to assert dominance.

- *The Gossip:* Spreads rumors and fuels workplace drama.

- *The Naysayer:* Criticizes ideas and discourages innovation.

- *The Passive-Aggressive:* Expresses negativity indirectly, undermining teamwork.

- *The Perfectionist:* Sets unrealistic standards, leading to friction.

These different types of personalities are illustrated in the following diagram.

Figure 15.1 Toxic Personalities

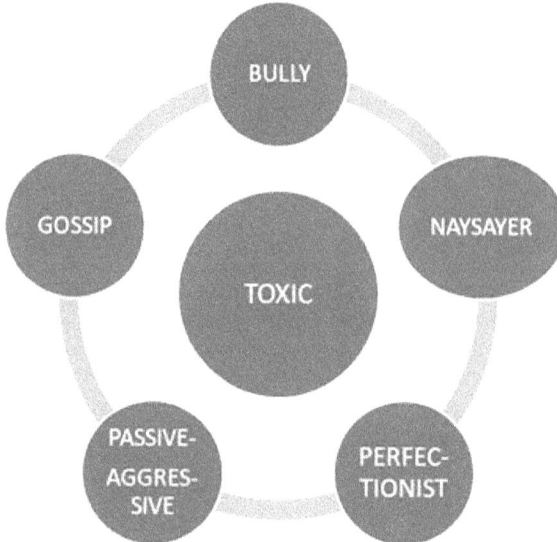

The Impact of Toxic Behaviors

Toxic behaviors have a variety of negative effects in the workplace. Among them are:

- Reduced morale and collaboration.

- Increased stress and absenteeism.

- Declines in team productivity and trust.

Addressing Toxic Behaviors

The adage, "An ounce of prevention is better than a pound of cure" holds true in the case of toxic behaviors. However, it sometimes happens, for one reason or another, that behaviors become toxic and need to be addressed. To effectively address toxic behaviors, supervisors should:

- Document incidents to ensure clarity and accuracy.

- Address the behavior privately, focusing on its impact rather than personal criticism.

- Set clear expectations for change and follow up on progress.

Example: A team member frequently dismisses others' ideas during meetings, stifling discussion. The supervisor addresses this behavior directly, explains its impact on team morale, and sets a goal for fostering a more inclusive dialogue.

Section 2: Strategies for Dealing with Difficult Team Members

There is hardly a supervisor who has not had to deal with one or more difficult team members. In this section, we offer some proven strategies for addressing the problem of difficult team members.

1. Communication is Key

- Use active listening to understand underlying issues.

- Maintain a calm, professional tone during discussions.

- Provide specific examples of problematic behavior to avoid ambiguity.

2. Encourage Self-Reflection

- Ask open-ended questions to prompt the individual to consider his/her behavior.

- Provide constructive feedback and actionable suggestions for improvement.

3. Set Boundaries and Expectations

- Develop clear guidelines for acceptable workplace behavior.

- Reinforce these expectations consistently and fairly across the team.

4. Foster Collaboration

- Pair difficult individuals with team members who model positive behavior.

- Emphasize shared goals to reduce friction and encourage teamwork.

Practical Application: Conduct role-playing exercises where team members practice resolving conflicts constructively, simulating real-life scenarios.

Section 3: Knowing How and When to Escalate Issues

An important supervisory skill is knowing how and when to escalate issues. The primary objective of this section is to provide that information. We discuss when to escalate, how to escalate, and how to support the team during escalation.

1. When to Escalate

The supervisor should escalate the issue when:

- The behavior persists despite multiple interventions.

- The situation negatively affects the team or organization.

- The issue involves harassment, discrimination, or unethical conduct.

2. How to Escalate Professionally

Once the decision to escalate the issue has been made to escalate the issue, the supervisor should then:

- Follow organizational protocols for reporting and addressing issues.

- Provide detailed documentation, including dates, times, and specific incidents.

- Maintain confidentiality and professionalism during escalation.

3. Supporting the Team During Escalation

During escalation, the team needs support. To offer this support:

- Communicate transparently about steps being taken, without breaching confidentiality.

- Provide reassurance to affected team members.

- Monitor team morale and address concerns promptly.

Example: A supervisor repeatedly addresses disruptive behavior from a team member without success. Following policy, the issue is escalated to HR, ensuring proper resolution while minimizing the impact on the team.

Section 4: Building a Collaborative and Respectful Team Culture

Most supervisors, if given the choice, would choose a collaborative and respectful team over one that is prone to exhibiting toxic behaviors. The question is, how do we build a collaborative and respectful team culture? The answer is, by promoting mutual respect, establishing accountability, and providing ongoing training. Let's take a brief look at each of these measures:

1. Promoting Mutual Respect

- Model respectful behavior as a leader.

- Encourage open and respectful communication during conflicts.

2. Establishing Accountability

- Hold everyone accountable for his/her actions, regardless of seniority or tenure.

- Recognize and reward positive behaviors that align with team values.

3. Providing Ongoing Training

- Offer workshops on conflict resolution and communication skills.

- Use team-building activities to strengthen relationships and foster understanding.

Practical Application: Organize a team retreat to discuss shared values and establish ground rules for collaboration.

Key Takeaways

- Difficult personalities and situations can disrupt team harmony and productivity if not managed effectively.

- Supervisors must focus on addressing behaviors rather than personal traits.

- Clear communication, consistency, and fairness are essential in managing challenging situations.

- Escalating issues should be a last resort but must be done when necessary to protect the team's well-being and integrity.

Reflection Questions

1. How do you currently handle difficult personalities or situations on your team?

2. What strategies could you use to address toxic behaviors more effectively?

3. How can you balance fairness and accountability when dealing with challenging team dynamics?

Practical Applications and Exercises

1. Case Study Analysis
   - *Objective:* Analyze and resolve hypothetical workplace scenarios.

   - *Activity:* Present a scenario involving a difficult personality or situation. Ask participants to identify key issues and propose solutions.

2. Role-Playing Conflict Resolution
   - *Objective:* Build skills in addressing challenging behaviors.

- *Activity:* Pair team members to role-play supervisor-employee interactions, focusing on constructive feedback and problem-solving.

3. Team Agreement on Values
    - *Objective:* Foster a culture of respect and collaboration.

    - *Activity:* Facilitate a discussion where team members collectively define their core values and expectations for behavior.

Managing difficult personalities and situations is one of the most challenging aspects of supervision, but it is also one of the most rewarding when handled well. By addressing toxic behaviors, fostering open communication, and knowing when to escalate issues, supervisors can maintain a positive work environment that supports team morale and productivity. Mastering these skills ensures that you can lead with confidence and guide your team through even the toughest interpersonal challenges.

QUIZ FOR PART V

Indicate whether the following statements are true (T) or (F).

1. Remote and hybrid teams are similar in all respects. T   F

2. Remote and hybrid teams need no supervision. T   F

3. Technology can help supervisors manage remote and hybrid teams.   T   F

4. Video conferencing is a tool that can level the playing field for remote workers.   T   F

5. Proximity bias is the tendency to favor people who are physically close.   T   F

6. A unified culture can drive success.   T   F

7. Fatigue is never a sign of stress. T   F

8. One-on-one discussions can provide emotional support.   T   F

9. Bullies, as well as perfectionists, are toxic personalities.   T   F

10. Escalating issues should be a last resort.   T   F

ANSWERS

1 F   2 F   3 T   4 T   5 T   6 T   7 F   8 T
9 T   10 T

PART VI
SUPERVISING IN
SPECIAL SITUATIONS

CHAPTER 16
SUPERVISING TECHNICAL AND HIGHLY EDUCATED PEOPLE

Chapter Overview

Managing technical and highly educated professionals requires a thoughtful approach that respects their expertise, promotes collaboration, and maintains accountability. This chapter delves into the unique challenges of supervising such individuals, offering strategies to build trust, facilitate innovation, and communicate effectively. By leveraging their knowledge and skills, supervisors can foster an environment where both the team and the organization thrive.

Key Learning Objectives

By the end of this chapter, you should be able to:

1. Recognize the motivations and working dynamics of technical and highly educated professionals.

2. Apply strategies to build trust and credibility as a supervisor.

3. Facilitate collaboration and innovation within your team.

4. Implement effective communication techniques tailored to technical environments.

5. Balance team autonomy with organizational accountability.

Section 1. Understanding Technical and Highly Educated Teams

Highly educated professionals are often specialists in their fields, valuing autonomy, intellectual engagement, and meaningful contributions. Supervising them requires a leadership approach that goes beyond traditional methods. Supervisors must:

Respect Their Expertise

These team members have expended time, effort, and other resources to reach their positions. Recognize their knowledge and seek their input in decision-making. They have much to contribute. Avoid micromanagement, which can undermine their confidence and morale.

Value Intrinsic Motivation

These professionals are often driven by curiosity and the desire to solve problems. Align their tasks with their interests and organizational goals.

Balance Structure and Freedom

Provide clear objectives but allow flexibility in how they achieve them. Remember that there are many avenues to accomplish a goal.

Section 2. Building Trust and Establishing Credibility

Earning the trust of technical teams is vital to effective supervision. Trust is built on mutual respect, transparency, and consistent support. It is often the case that supervisors are not as knowledgeable in a particular field as some team members. In such cases, be honest about your knowledge limitations. Your role as a supervisor is to facilitate, not to compete with their expertise.

Team members with a certain level of expertise and education have the ability to make certain technical decisions. Give them the autonomy to make technical decisions while maintaining oversight of broader objectives. By doing so, you are demonstrating that you value their expertise. Advocate for the needs of technical and highly educated teams by ensuring they have the resources, training, and tools they need to perform their roles effectively.

Section 3. Encouraging Collaboration and Innovation

Technical and highly educated teams often thrive when they are encouraged to collaborate and innovate. Your role as a supervisor is to create an environment that supports these efforts. You can create such an environment by:

(a) Fostering a culture of open communication. Encourage team members to share ideas and challenge assumptions without fear of judgment;

(b) Supporting risk-taking. Emphasize that failure is part of the innovation process. Celebrate learning from setbacks as much as successes;

(c) Facilitating interdisciplinary collaboration. Create opportunities for technical professionals to work with other departments, broadening perspectives and enhancing teamwork.

Section 4. Addressing Common Challenges in Supervising Experts

Managing technical and highly educated teams comes with unique challenges, from addressing intellectual egos to ensuring alignment with organizational goals. Supervisors must balance independence and accountability, resolve conflicts among experts, and manage resistance to change. Let us look briefly at each challenge.

Balancing Independence and Accountability

While autonomy is important, supervisors should set clear expectations and regularly review progress to ensure alignment. Balancing independence and accountability is about fostering an environment where individuals have the freedom to innovate and make decisions while remaining responsible for their actions and outcomes. This equilibrium ensures both personal growth and organizational success, creating a culture of trust and reliability.

Resolving Conflicts Among Experts

Disagreements may arise over technical approaches. Act as a mediator to guide discussions toward consensus.

Resolving conflicts among experts requires fostering respectful dialogue, focusing on shared goals, and facilitating collaborative problem-solving to leverage their diverse perspectives constructively.

Managing Resistance to Change

Highly educated professionals can sometimes be resistant to altering established methods. Engage them in the change process early, explaining the rationale and seeking their input. If they feel that they are a part of the process, they are more likely to support the change and work toward its success.

Section 5. Communicating Effectively with Technical Teams

Clear communication is essential for supervising technical professionals, especially when bridging the gap between technical and non-technical stakeholders. When communicating with technical and highly educated team members, the following points should be kept in mind: adapt your language, encourage two-way dialogue, and clarify goals and expectations. We will briefly address each point.

Adapt Your Language

Use plain terms when communicating with broader audiences but maintain technical depth when discussing details with the team. When communicating with technical and highly educated team members, your aim is to understand and to be understood, not to impress.

Encourage Two-Way Dialogue

Create an open environment where team members feel comfortable asking questions and offering feedback. Remember the role of feedback in the communication model presented in Chapter 4.

Clarify Goals and Expectations

Ensure alignment by regularly reiterating the broader vision and how the team's work contributes to it. Technical and highly educated team members are motivated by knowing they are a part of something worthwhile.

Key Takeaways

- Respect for expertise and autonomy is central to leading technical teams.

- Trust is built through transparency, empowerment, and consistent support.

- Collaboration and innovation thrive in environments that embrace open communication and calculated risk-taking.

- Effective communication bridges the gap between technical depth and organizational goals.

- Balancing independence with accountability ensures that team efforts align with the larger mission.

Reflection Questions

1. How do you currently demonstrate respect for the expertise of your team members?

2. What steps can you take to build stronger trust with your team?

3. How do you encourage collaboration and innovation in your team's projects?

4. What strategies do you use to balance autonomy and accountability?

5. How can you improve communication with both technical and non-technical stakeholders?

Practical Application Exercises

1. **Autonomy and Accountability Worksheet:** List tasks or projects where team members could benefit from more autonomy. Identify areas where closer oversight is required and establish clear accountability measures.

2. **Facilitated Innovation Session:** Organize a brainstorming session where team members present creative solutions to a current challenge. Document and follow up on actionable ideas.

3. **Conflict Resolution Simulation:** Role-play a scenario where two team members disagree on a technical solution. Practice mediating the discussion to reach a collaborative resolution.

4. **Feedback Framework Development:** Create a system for collecting and implementing team feedback on projects and workplace dynamics.

5. **Communication Style Review:** Analyze recent interactions with your team. Identify opportunities

to adjust your communication style for improved clarity and engagement.

Supervising technical and highly educated professionals is both challenging and rewarding. By respecting their expertise, fostering collaboration, and maintaining open communication, you can inspire your team to achieve excellence. As you implement the strategies in this chapter, remember that effective leadership is about empowering your team to succeed, both individually and collectively, within the organization's goals.

CHAPTER 17
SUPERVISING IN
THE PUBLIC SECTOR

Chapter Overview

Supervising in the public sector presents both unique challenges and significant opportunities. Unlike the private sector, public sector supervisors must maneuver complex bureaucratic systems, adhere to strict regulations, and maintain transparency and accountability to the public. These responsibilities are further compounded by the mission-driven nature of public service and the need to lead diverse teams often motivated by values rather than profit. This chapter delves deeply into the dynamics of supervising in the public sector, offering practical strategies for handling bureaucracy, fostering accountability, motivating teams, and aligning efforts with organizational and societal goals.

Key Learning Objectives

By the end of this chapter, you should be able to:

1. Understand the distinct characteristics of public sector supervision.

2. Handle bureaucratic systems and comply with regulations effectively.

3. Foster a culture of accountability and transparency.

4. Motivate and manage diverse teams within a public service framework.

5. Align team efforts with the broader mission of public service.

Section 1: Understanding the Public Sector Environment

Supervising in the public sector requires an awareness of its distinctive environment, which is shaped by the overarching goal of serving the public good. Supervisors must be aware of the following aspects of the public sector.

Mission-Driven Work

Public sector organizations are fundamentally driven by a commitment to societal impact. Unlike private companies focused on profits, public sector entities prioritize the welfare of individuals and communities. As a supervisor, you must keep this mission at the forefront, ensuring that your team understands how its work contributes to a larger purpose. For example, a public health department supervisor can inspire its team by connecting daily tasks to the broader goal of improving community health outcomes.

Complex Bureaucracy

Bureaucratic systems, while often criticized, are designed to ensure fairness, accountability, and consistency. Supervisors must manage these systems effectively, understanding the policies, procedures, and hierarchical structures that guide decision-making. For instance, securing funding for a new initiative may require adhering to detailed protocols and obtaining multiple approvals. Understanding these processes allows supervisors to anticipate challenges and act strategically.

Public Scrutiny

Public sector supervisors must operate with an awareness that their actions are subject to substantial scrutiny. Decisions must not only be legally compliant but also ethically sound and defensible in the public eye. Transparency is essential, as stakeholders, including taxpayers, media, and advocacy groups, may demand explanations for how resources are allocated and managed.

Section 2: Navigating Bureaucracy and Regulations

Effective supervision in the public sector depends on mastering the art of maneuvering bureaucracy without becoming bogged down by it.

Mastering Procedures

Supervisors should invest time in understanding the policies and regulations that govern their organization.

This knowledge allows them to act with confidence and efficiency. For instance, a supervisor in a municipal government might streamline procurement processes by knowing which approvals can be expedited and which must follow a strict timeline.

Effective Decision-Making

Balancing procedural compliance with the need for timely decisions is a critical skill. Supervisors must learn when to seek additional approvals and when to proceed within their authority. This often involves weighing risks against potential benefits while maintaining transparency.

Advocating for Resources

Public sector supervisors often face resource constraints. Advocacy skills are crucial for securing funding, staffing, and tools needed to support their teams. By presenting data-driven arguments and aligning requests with organizational priorities, supervisors can increase the likelihood of receiving support.

Section 3: Building Accountability and Transparency

A culture of accountability ensures that public sector teams operate with integrity and efficiency, maintaining public trust. Building a culture of accountability involves setting clear expectations, regular reporting, and ethical leadership.

Clear Expectations

Accountability begins with clear communication. Supervisors should establish measurable goals and articulate expectations. For instance, a supervisor in a public works department might set specific targets for road maintenance projects, such as completing repairs within a set timeframe and budget.

Regular Reporting

Regularly documenting and sharing progress fosters a sense of responsibility. Supervisors can implement tools like project management software or team dashboards to track milestones and identify potential delays. Regular reporting also gives the impression of openness.

Ethical Leadership

Supervisors set the tone for accountability through their actions. Demonstrating fairness, consistency, and ethical decision-making builds trust within the team and with stakeholders.

Section 4: Motivating and Managing Diverse Teams

Diversity in the public sector workforce mirrors the communities served, making inclusive leadership essential.

Understanding Motivations

Public sector employees are often motivated by a desire to contribute to societal well-being. Recognizing and affirming these values can inspire teams to perform at their best. For example, a supervisor in an environmental agency might highlight how individual contributions support sustainable practices that benefit future generations.

Conflict Resolution

Conflicts in diverse teams can arise from differing perspectives or misunderstandings. Supervisors must address these issues promptly, fostering open dialogue and equitable solutions. For instance, organizing mediation sessions can help resolve disputes while maintaining team cohesion.

Professional Development

Investing in employee growth is key to long-term motivation. Supervisors should identify training opportunities, encourage participation in skill-building workshops, and support career advancement within the organization.

Section 5: Aligning Efforts with the Public Service Mission

The ultimate responsibility of public sector supervisors is to ensure that their team's work aligns with the broader goals of the organization. They do this by communicating the organization's vision, engaging stakeholders, and adapting to change. We comment on each in turn.

Communicating the Vision

Supervisors must consistently reinforce the connection between daily tasks and the organization's mission.

Sharing success stories or milestones achieved can help team members see the tangible impact of their efforts.

Engaging Stakeholders

Collaboration is often necessary to achieve public service goals. Supervisors should build relationships with other departments, external agencies, and community groups to align efforts and share resources to the extent possible.

Adapting to Change

Policy changes, budget adjustments, and emerging public needs require supervisors to remain flexible. By staying informed and proactive, supervisors can guide their teams through transitions with minimal disruption.

Key Takeaways

- Supervising in the public sector requires balancing procedural compliance with team leadership.

- Accountability and transparency are critical to maintaining public trust.

- Understanding and leveraging the motivations of a diverse workforce fosters engagement and productivity.

- Aligning team efforts with organizational missions amplifies public service impact.

Reflection Questions

1. How does the mission-driven nature of the public sector influence your supervisory approach?

2. What strategies can you use to handle bureaucratic challenges effectively?

3. How do you promote accountability and transparency within your team?

4. In what ways can you support and motivate a diverse workforce?

5. How do you ensure that your team's efforts align with the larger public service goals?

Practical Application Exercises

1. Policy Familiarization Challenge: Identify a policy or regulation relevant to your team. Create a brief guide explaining its purpose and implementation.

2. Accountability Framework Development: Design a simple system for tracking team progress toward goals, incorporating regular feedback and reporting mechanisms.

3. Motivation Mapping Exercise: Survey your team members to understand their motivations and values. Use the results to tailor recognition and development opportunities.

4. Stakeholder Collaboration Role-Play: Simulate a scenario where your team collaborates with another department or external agency. Practice

strategies for effective communication and alignment.

5. Public Service Alignment Plan: Create a plan that outlines how your team's work supports the organizational mission and benefits the public. Present it in a team meeting to inspire alignment and focus.

Supervising in the public sector requires a blend of strategic navigation, ethical leadership, and people management skills. By embracing the unique challenges and opportunities of this environment, supervisors can inspire their teams to achieve meaningful outcomes. Ultimately, their leadership not only drives organizational success but also contributes to the greater good, leaving a lasting impact on the communities they serve.

QUIZ FOR PART VI

1. Technical and highly educated professionals don't need to be motivated. T   F

2. Technical and highly educated professionals value autonomy.   T   F

3. Technical and highly educated professionals are often driven by curiosity.   T   F

4. Supervisors can safely ignore trust issues when dealing with technical and highly educated teams. T   F

5. Balancing independence with accountability does not apply to highly educated professionals.   T   F

6. Respect for expertise and autonomy is central to leading highly educated professionals.   T   F

7. Supervising in the public sector is no different from supervising in the private sector.   T   F

8. The objective of public sector organizations is to maximize profits.   T   F

9. Public   sector   supervisors   often   face   resource constraints.   T   F

10. Public sector workforces are likely to be more diverse than uniform.   T   F

ANSWERS

1 F   2 T   3 T   4 F   5 F   6 T   7 F   8 F
9 T   10 T

PART VII
SUPERVISING FOR
THE FUTURE

CHAPTER 18
ETHICAL SUPERVISION AND INTEGRITY IN LEADERSHIP

Chapter Overview

Ethics and integrity are not just abstract ideals; they are the foundation upon which effective supervision is built. As a supervisor, your commitment to ethical principles shapes the culture of your team and sets the standard for the organization. Ethical leadership is about more than avoiding misconduct—it is about actively promoting trust, fairness, and accountability.

This chapter delves into the essence of ethical supervision, exploring its significance, the challenges that often arise, and practical strategies for addressing complex situations with integrity. By understanding and embodying these principles, supervisors can create an environment where every team member feels valued and respected, while the organization flourishes through a shared commitment to doing what is right.

Key Learning Objectives

By the end of this chapter, you should be able to:

1. Understand the critical role ethics and integrity play in effective supervision.

2. Identify and address common ethical challenges in the workplace with confidence.

3. Apply practical tools to foster a workplace culture grounded in ethical behavior.

4. Lead by example, demonstrating fairness, transparency, and accountability.

5. Deal with ethical dilemmas while upholding professional and organizational standards.

Section 1:
The Foundations of Ethical Supervision

Defining Ethical Leadership

Ethical leadership is about consistently doing the right thing, even when it is inconvenient or difficult. It involves acting with integrity, honesty, and fairness while prioritizing the well-being of your team and organization. Ethical supervisors do not merely enforce rules; they embody the values that the organization upholds, serving as role models for their teams.

Why Ethics Matter

Ethical behavior in leadership has far-reaching consequences. When team members trust that their supervisor will act fairly and transparently, they feel more secure and engaged. This trust not only enhances team morale but also strengthens the organization's reputation. Moreover, ethical supervision reduces the risk of misconduct and legal issues, promoting long-term stability and success.

Core Principles of Ethical Supervision

Before we delve more deeply into ethical supervision, let us consider its core principles. They are:

1. **Honesty:** Always communicate openly and truthfully, even when the truth is difficult to hear.

2. **Fairness:** Treat all team members equitably, avoiding favoritism or bias.

3. **Respect:** Value diverse perspectives and contributions, ensuring that every voice is heard.

4. **Accountability:** Accept responsibility for your actions and decisions, and expect the same from your team.

These core principles are illustrated in Figure 16.1 below.

Figure 16.1 Core Principles of Ethical Supervision

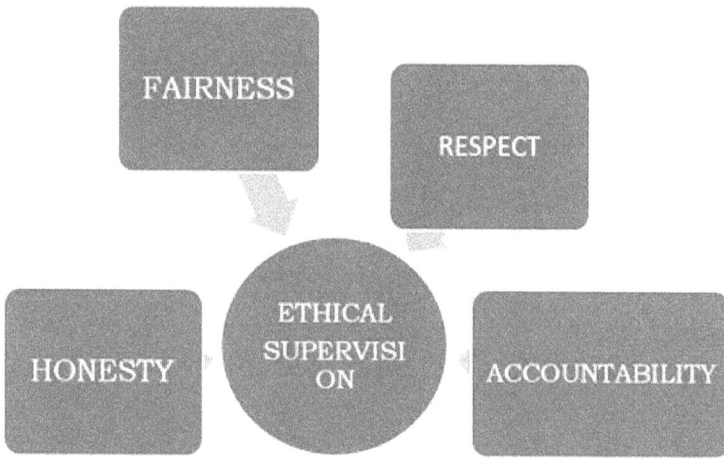

Section 2: Recognizing and Addressing Ethical Challenges

Common Ethical Challenges

Even the most principled supervisors will face ethical dilemmas. Some of the most common challenges include:

Conflicts of interest: Situations where personal relationships or potential gains might influence decision-making.

Favoritism: Unequal treatment of team members, whether intentional or accidental.

Breaches of Confidentiality: Inappropriate sharing of sensitive information.

Misuse of resources: Personal use of organizational assets, such as funds, equipment, or time.

Strategies for Addressing Ethical Dilemmas

Ethical challenges often present a test of character. When faced with such situations, the supervisor should:

Consult policies and codes of conduct: Your organization's guidelines provide a framework for decision-making.

Seek advice: Turn to mentors, HR professionals, or ethics committees for guidance.

Prioritize integrity: Focus on long-term outcomes rather than short-term convenience or gain.

Example: Imagine a high-performing team member who violates a procedural rule. While his/her contributions are valuable, overlooking that individual's misconduct could undermine team morale and set a dangerous precedent. By addressing the issue fairly and transparently, you uphold the organization's standards while fostering trust and accountability.

Section 3: Creating and Sustaining an Ethical Workplace Culture

Establishing Clear Ethical Guidelines

Clear expectations are essential for maintaining integrity within a team. Supervisors should:

(a) Develop and communicate a code of ethics tailored to the team's needs.

(b) Provide training sessions to ensure team members understand ethical principles and how to apply them.

Encouraging Open Communication

An ethical culture thrives when employees feel safe to speak up. Supervisors should therefore:

(a) Foster an open-door policy where concerns can be raised without fear of retaliation.

(b) Protect whistle-blowers to encourage transparency and accountability.

Reinforcing Ethical Behavior

Recognizing and rewarding ethical conduct is just as important as addressing misconduct. Supervisors can:

- Publicly acknowledge team members who demonstrate integrity.

- Take swift, consistent action when unethical behavior arises.

Practical Application: Host a team workshop where employees discuss ethical scenarios and collaborate to develop appropriate solutions. This exercise promotes shared understanding and reinforces the team's commitment to ethical values.

Section 4: Leading by Example

Modeling Integrity in Leadership

As a supervisor, your actions speak louder than your words. To provide ethical leadership:

- *Be transparent:* Share the rationale behind your decisions to build trust.

- *Own your mistakes:* Admitting errors demonstrates accountability and encourages others to do the same.

- *Avoid double standards:* Hold yourself to the same expectations as your team.

Building Trust Through Ethical Leadership

Trust is the cornerstone of effective supervision. By consistently demonstrating fairness, empathy, and reliability, you create a foundation of mutual respect that empowers your team to excel.

Example: A supervisor realizes that a scheduling error has created conflicts among team members. By openly acknowledging the mistake, apologizing, and taking corrective action, the supervisor strengthens trust and demonstrates accountability.

Key Takeaways

- Ethical supervision fosters trust, credibility, and a positive work environment.

- Leading by example is the most effective way to instill integrity in your team.

- Transparency and fairness are critical to resolving ethical challenges effectively.

- Clear ethical guidelines and open communication help prevent misconduct and strengthen accountability.

Practical Applications and Exercises

1. **Case Study Analysis**
   - Consider a scenario involving an ethical dilemma.
   - Identify the ethical principles at stake and propose a course of action.

2. **Personal Reflection on Integrity**
   - Complete a self-assessment questionnaire on ethical leadership practices. See Appendix B.
   - Reflect on areas where you can enhance your alignment with core principles.

3. **Team Ethics Charter**
   - Collaborate with your team to draft a charter that outlines shared ethical values and behavioral standards.

Reflection Questions

1. How do your personal values align with your role as a supervisor?

2. Have you encountered an ethical challenge in the workplace, and how did you address it?

3. What steps can you take to foster greater accountability and integrity within your team?

Ethical supervision is not just about avoiding wrongdoing; it is about creating an environment where integrity and accountability are celebrated. By leading with fairness, transparency, and respect, you not only set a standard for your team but also contribute to the long-term success of your organization.

In the next chapter, *The Evolving Role of Supervisors in a Changing Workplace*, we will explore how supervisors can adapt to dynamic organizational needs, emerging technologies, and shifting employee expectations to remain effective leaders in today's ever-changing world.

CHAPTER 19
THE EVOLVING ROLE OF SUPERVISORS IN A CHANGING WORKPLACE

Chapter Overview

The workplace is undergoing rapid transformation, driven by advances in technology, shifts in employee expectations, and an increasingly diverse workforce. Supervisors must adapt to these changes by rethinking traditional leadership strategies and acquiring new skills to remain effective.

This final chapter explores the trends shaping the supervisory role, outlines essential skills for the future, and provides strategies for preparing both yourself and your team for ongoing change. It concludes by emphasizing the importance of adaptability, innovation, and resilience in mastering this evolving landscape.

Key Learning Objectives

By the end of this chapter, you should be able to:

1. Recognize the key trends impacting the role of supervisors in today's workplace.

2. Develop future-ready supervisory skills to effectively lead diverse and dynamic teams.

3. Prepare yourself and your team to embrace and deal with change.

4. Foster a resilient, inclusive, and future-oriented team culture.

Section 1: The Transformative Trends Impacting Supervisory Roles

Supervisors are at the forefront of adapting to workplace transformations. The following trends are reshaping their roles:

Artificial Intelligence (AI) and Automation

Technology is automating repetitive tasks, increasing productivity, and requiring supervisors to guide teams through technological transitions. Key responsibilities include:

(a) Integrating AI and automation tools into workflows.

(b) Supporting team members in acquiring new, tech-relevant skills.

Diversity, Equity, and Inclusion (DEI)

As workplaces become more diverse, supervisors play a critical role in fostering inclusivity. Supervisors should:

(a) Recognize and address unconscious biases.

(b) Create a culture where all team members feel valued and respected.

Employee Expectations in a Hybrid World

The rise of remote and hybrid work models has changed how employees perceive flexibility, productivity, and work-life balance. Supervisors must therefore:

(a) Adapt to managing distributed teams while maintaining team cohesion.

(b) Be attuned to the mental health and well-being of their team members.

Section 2: Supervisory Skills for the Future

To thrive in this new environment, supervisors must cultivate a mix of technical and interpersonal skills.

Emotional Intelligence (EI)

In Section 1, we briefly discussed artificial intelligence (AI). Now, we will pay some attention to emotional intelligence (EI). Effective supervisors understand and regulate emotions—both their own and their team's. This includes:

(a) Developing empathy and active listening skills.

(b) Managing conflicts and promoting harmonious relationships.

Technological Proficiency

Supervisors need to understand workplace technologies and leverage them effectively. Key practices include:

(a) Familiarity with collaboration platforms and AI-driven tools.

(b) Staying informed about technological advancements relevant to their industry.

Adaptability and Resilience

Supervisors must set an example by embracing change. To do this, they should:

- Stay flexible in the face of uncertainty.

- Help their teams view change as an opportunity for growth.

Inclusive Leadership

Creating a space where diverse voices are heard and appreciated is essential. In this regard, supervisors need to:

- Build diverse teams and leverage their strengths.

- Encourage open dialogue and equitable decision-making.

Section 3: Preparing Yourself and Your Team for Change

The Greek philosopher Heraclitus of Ephesus is credited with saying, "The only constant in life is change". Change is something that we must learn to accept and cope with.

Continuous Learning and Development

The rapidly changing workplace demands ongoing skill-building. Supervisors can:

- Pursue professional development opportunities like training or certifications.

- Encourage their teams to develop skills aligned with future needs.

Effective Change Management

Supervisors must guide their teams through change with clarity and support. Strategies to effectively achieve this include:

- Communicating openly about the reasons for and benefits of change.

- Empowering team members to contribute to solutions during transitions.

Building a Resilient Team Culture

Teams thrive in environments where they feel supported during change. Supervisors can foster resilience by:

- Recognizing team achievements during challenging periods.

- Offering resources such as mentorship programs or wellness initiatives.

Section 4:
Leading with Vision and Innovation

Anticipating the Future

Great supervisors anticipate changes and proactively position their teams for success. They achieve this by doing the following two things:

(1) Keeping abreast of industry trends and market shifts.

(2) Encouraging innovative thinking and creative problem-solving within their teams.

Cultivating a Growth Mindset

Supervisors who embrace a growth mindset inspire their teams to see challenges as opportunities. To accomplish this, supervisors should:

- Encourage experimentation and learning from mistakes.
- Celebrate progress, no matter how small.

Balancing Stability with Flexibility

While change is inevitable, supervisors must provide a sense of stability to their teams. Strategies to provide stability include:

- Maintaining clear goals and priorities during periods of uncertainty.
- Being open to adjusting plans as new information arises.

Key Takeaways

- **Adaptability is Essential:** As workplaces undergo rapid changes, supervisors must remain flexible and open to continuous learning to effectively address new challenges and opportunities.

- **Technological Proficiency is Critical:** Understanding and leveraging workplace technologies are crucial for enhancing team collaboration, productivity, and efficiency in hybrid and remote settings.

- **Emphasis on Emotional Intelligence:** Supervisors must strengthen their emotional intelligence to connect with employees, manage stress, and foster a supportive work environment amid uncertainties.

- **Cultivating a Growth Mindset:** Encouraging innovation, skill development, and resilience within teams helps employees stay engaged and relevant in a fast-changing workplace.

- **Championing Diversity and Inclusion:** Supervisors play a key role in creating an equitable workplace by addressing biases, fostering cultural awareness, and promoting inclusive practices.

- **Balancing Flexibility and Accountability:** As flexible work arrangements become the norm, supervisors must skillfully balance granting autonomy with maintaining high-performance standards.

- **Leading Through Change:** Supervisors should act as change agents, guiding their teams through organizational transformations with clarity, empathy, and strategic communication.

- **Focus on Employee Well-being:** Supervisors must prioritize the physical and mental health of their teams, ensuring that workplace practices promote a holistic sense of well-being.

- **Reinforcing Core Leadership Principles:** Amid evolving expectations, the timeless principles of clear communication, trust-building, and ethical leadership remain vital to supervisory success.

- **Preparing for Future Trends:** Staying informed about emerging workplace trends and preparing for their implications ensures supervisors can lead effectively in an ever-changing environment.

Practical Applications and Exercises

1. Trend Analysis Exercise

Identify one trend (e.g., AI, diversity, hybrid work) impacting your workplace. Discuss its implications with your team and brainstorm strategies to adapt it effectively.

2. Skill Development Plan

Conduct a self-assessment and team assessment to identify skill gaps.

Develop a roadmap for acquiring or enhancing these skills over the next year.

Scenario Planning Workshop

Engage your team in a workshop to explore possible future scenarios (e.g., new technologies or organizational changes). Plan how to address these scenarios successfully.

Reflection Questions

1. How are you currently adapting to the trends shaping today's workplace?

2. What future-ready skills do you need to develop to remain effective as a supervisor?

3. How can you foster a team culture that embraces change and innovation?

The role of supervisors is evolving rapidly, shaped by technological advancements, workforce diversity, and changing employee expectations. By understanding these trends, developing essential skills, and preparing your team for the future, you can remain a confident and effective leader in any environment.

This chapter concludes the journey through *Mastering Supervisory Excellence*. As you move forward, remember that supervision is an ever-changing craft requiring adaptability, curiosity, and a commitment to growth.

QUIZ FOR PART VII

Indicate whether the following statements are true (T) or false (F).

1. Ethical leadership is about maximizing the satisfaction of the majority of people.   T   F

2. Ethical supervisors engender security.   T   F

3. Honesty and fairness are core principles of ethical supervision.   T   F

4. Favoritism is not an ethical challenge.   T   F

5. Whistle-blowers are toxic and not to be protected.   T   F

6. Leading by example is an effective way to instill integrity in team members.   T   F

7. Supervisors should always resist artificial intelligence (AI) and automation because they cause unemployment.   T   F

8. Supervisors should keep abreast of industry trends.   T   F

9. Unfortunately, supervisors cannot be change agents.   T   F

10. Emotional intelligence (EI) is obsolete in the modern workplace.   T   F

ANSWERS

1 F   2 T   3 T   4 F   5 F   6 T   7 F   8 T
9 F   10 F

CONCLUSION

As we conclude this journey through *Mastering Supervisory Excellence*, it's important to reflect on the key principles that have guided this exploration of supervisory skills. Being a supervisor is more than a position—it is a responsibility to lead, inspire, and empower others. The chapters you have just read offer a comprehensive framework, but true success as a supervisor lies not only in mastering a set of skills but also in embracing a mindset of growth and continuous learning.

Becoming a Continuous Learner: Staying Relevant and Up-to-Date in Supervisory Skills

The landscape of leadership and management is constantly evolving. Technological advancements, shifting team dynamics, and changing organizational priorities require supervisors to stay agile, adaptable, and proactive. Becoming a continuous learner is not optional in today's fast-paced, globalized workplace—it's essential for long-term success.

To stay relevant, supervisors must engage in ongoing development—whether through reading the latest leadership books, attending webinars, taking online courses, or participating in professional networks. Just as you encourage your team to grow and develop, you too must invest in your personal growth. By embracing a lifelong learning mindset, you can remain a valuable asset to your team and organization, regardless of the changes that come your way.

Here are a few strategies to help maintain your relevance as a supervisor:

Stay Curious: Ask questions, seek feedback, and never assume that you have all the answers.

Pursue Professional Development: Regularly update your knowledge and skills through formal education, peer learning, and leadership workshops.

Leverage Technology: Stay abreast of new tools and technologies that can help streamline processes, enhance communication, and improve team collaboration.

Embrace Change: Adaptability is one of the most important traits of a successful supervisor. Be willing to experiment with new approaches and be open to feedback.

By committing to your own growth, you'll not only lead by example but also set the stage for continued success as the work environment continues to change.

Final Thoughts on
Building a Successful Supervisory Career

Building a successful supervisory career is not a destination but a journey. It's not about reaching a final "perfect" stage, but rather about continuously evolving and responding to new challenges. As you grow in your role, the nature of your relationships with your team, your ability to influence positive outcomes, and your capacity to inspire others will deepen.

Successful supervisors are not just managers—they are mentors, coaches, and facilitators. They create environments where people can thrive, communicate openly, and work together toward a common goal. The best supervisors understand the value of empathy and emotional intelligence, how to nurture trust within teams, and the power of encouragement and recognition. They recognize that leadership is ultimately about serving those they lead.

Here are a few guiding principles to keep in mind as you build your career:

Lead with Integrity: Your actions as a supervisor will always speak louder than your words. Demonstrating honesty, transparency, and fairness builds trust and credibility with your team.

Develop Strong Relationships: Connect with your team members on both a professional and human level. Show genuine interest in their growth and well-being.

Foster a Positive Culture: Cultivate a culture of respect, recognition, and inclusivity. When people feel valued and supported, they perform at their best.

Be a Change Agent: Embrace change and position yourself as a leader who helps guide teams through transitions with confidence and optimism.

Invest in Your Team: Equip your team members with the tools, knowledge, and support they need to succeed. Their success is your success.

Remember, supervisory excellence doesn't happen overnight. It requires patience, persistence, and a commitment to continuous improvement. By honing your leadership skills and consistently striving to elevate those around you, you'll build a supervisory career that is both fulfilling and impactful.

Looking Ahead

As you embark on the next phase of your supervisory journey, continue to seek opportunities for growth, feedback, and reflection. The principles outlined in this book are only the beginning. The true mark of excellence is not just the ability to manage—it's the capacity to inspire, motivate, and cultivate an environment where both individuals and teams can flourish.

May you continue to grow as a leader, create meaningful change in your organization, and lead with the same passion, integrity, and commitment that will define you as an exceptional supervisor for years to come.

Best of luck on your journey toward mastering supervisory excellence!

APPENDICES

APPENDIX A: SAMPLE TEMPLATES AND CHECKLISTS

APPENDIX B: RECOMMENDED RESOURCES FOR SUPERVISORS

APPENDIX C: SELF-ASSESSMENT QUESTIONNAIRE ON ETHICAL LEADERSHIP

APPENDIX A
SAMPLE TEMPLATES
AND CHECKLISTS

Performance Evaluation Template for Team Members

Employee Name: _____

Position/Title: _____

Department: _____

Evaluation Period: _____

Supervisor/Reviewer: _____

Section 1: Core Competencies

Rate the team member on a scale of 1–5, where:
1 = Needs Improvement | 2 = Fair | 3 = Satisfactory | 4 = Good | 5 = Excellent

Competency	Rating	Comments
Job Knowledge and Expertise		Demonstrates understanding and proficiency in job-related skills and tasks.
Quality of Work		Produces accurate, thorough, and high-quality results.
Productivity and Efficiency		Completes tasks within deadlines and manages time effectively.
Teamwork and		Works effectively with others and

Competency	Rating	Comments
Collaboration		contributes positively to team goals.
Communication Skills		Clearly expresses ideas and listens actively to others.
Problem-Solving and Initiative		Identifies issues, proposes solutions, and takes initiative when appropriate.
Adaptability		Adjusts well to changing priorities and environments.
Dependability and Reliability		Consistently fulfills responsibilities and meets commitments.
Professionalism and Work Ethic		Displays integrity, accountability, and a positive attitude.

Section 2: Goal Achievement

Evaluate the team member's progress toward individual and team goals during the evaluation period.

Goal Achieved (Y/N) Comments

Goal 1: _____

Goal 2: _____

Goal 3: _____

Section 3: Strengths and Development Areas

Strengths

Highlight key strengths demonstrated by the team member:

1. _____

2. _____

3. _____

Development Areas

Identify areas for improvement or growth:

1. _____

2. _____

3. _____

Section 4: Training and Development Recommendations

Suggest specific training, resources, or opportunities to enhance the team member's skills and performance:

1. _____

2. _____

3. _____

Section 5: Summary Evaluation

Overall Performance Rating

☐ Needs Improvement

☐ Fair

☐ Satisfactory

☐ Good

☐ Excellent

Narrative Summary

Provide a brief summary of the team member's overall performance:

_____

_____

_____

_____

Section 6: Employee Acknowledgment

Employee Comments (Optional):

_____

_____

Employee Signature: _____

Date: _____

Supervisor Signature: _____

Date: _____

Sample Goal-setting Worksheet

Name: _____

Position/Title: _____

Department: _____

Supervisor: _____

Date: _____

Step 1: Define Your Goal

Goal Title:

Goal Description:

Clearly outline the specific goal you want to achieve.

_____

_____

Why is this goal important?

Explain how achieving this goal aligns with organizational objectives or personal development.

_____

_____

_____

Step 2: Make Your Goal SMART

SMART goals are **Specific, Measurable, Achievable, Relevant**, and **Time-bound.**

SMART Element	Details
Specific:	What exactly do you want to accomplish?
Measurable:	How will you track progress and determine success?
Achievable:	Is this goal realistic and attainable?
Relevant:	How does this goal align with team/organizational priorities?
Time-bound:	What is the deadline for achieving this goal?

Step 3: Break Your Goal into Actionable Steps

List the steps you'll take to accomplish your goal.

Step	Description	Deadline	Resources/Support Needed
1			
2			
3			
4			

Step 4: Identify Potential Challenges and Solutions

Anticipate obstacles that might arise and plan how to address them.

Challenge	Proposed Solution
1	

2

3

Step 5: Set Evaluation Criteria

Determine how you will evaluate the success of your goal.

Metric/Indicator Target/Benchmark Evaluation Date

Step 6: Review and Reflect

Schedule periodic check-ins to assess progress and make adjustments.

Review Date Progress Notes Next Steps/Adjustments

Signature (Employee): _____

Signature (Supervisor): _____

Date: _____

Conflict Resolution Checklist

This checklist serves as a practical guide for supervisors to handle conflicts effectively while fostering a culture of collaboration and mutual respect.

Step 1: Prepare for Resolution

☐ Understand the Conflict

- Identify the root cause of the conflict (e.g., miscommunication, differing expectations).
- Gather relevant facts and perspectives from all parties involved.

☐ Evaluate Your Role

- Assess your neutrality and readiness to mediate.
- Reflect on any biases or assumptions you may have.

☐ Set the Environment

- Choose a neutral, private location for discussions.
- Ensure all participants feel safe and respected.

Step 2: Facilitate Open Communication

☐ Establish Ground Rules

- Encourage respectful behavior and active listening.
- Prohibit interruptions or aggressive language.

☐ Allow Each Party to Speak

- Provide equal time for each individual to share his/her perspective.

- Focus on understanding, not assigning blame.

☐ Clarify Issues

- Summarize and confirm key points shared by all parties.

- Ask open-ended questions to gather more information.

Step 3: Collaborate on Solutions

☐ Identify Common Goals

- Highlight shared objectives or values to create a foundation for resolution.

☐ Brainstorm Solutions

- Encourage all parties to suggest possible solutions.

- Evaluate the feasibility and fairness of each option.

☐ Agree on an Action Plan

- Define specific actions, responsibilities, and deadlines.

- Document the agreement for accountability.

Step 4: Implement and Follow Up

☐ Take Immediate Action

- Ensure all agreed-upon steps are implemented promptly.
- Provide any necessary support or resources.

☐ Monitor Progress

- Schedule follow-ups to review progress and address lingering concerns.

☐ Evaluate Outcomes

- Assess whether the conflict has been resolved effectively.
- Reflect on lessons learned to prevent similar conflicts in the future.

Step 5: Maintain a Positive Work Environment

☐ Promote Preventative Practices

- Foster open communication and regular check-ins with the team.
- Encourage team-building activities to strengthen relationships.

☐ Encourage Feedback

- Create a safe space for team members to voice concerns early.
- Act promptly to address minor issues before they escalate.

☐ Lead by Example

- Demonstrate fairness, respect, and a commitment to resolving conflicts constructively.

Signature (Supervisor): _____

Signature (Employee): _____

Date: _____

APPENDIX B
RECOMMENDED RESOURCES
FOR SUPERVISORS

*This appendix provides a curated list of resources to help supervisors enhance their skills and succeed in their leadership roles. These resources align with the principles outlined in **Mastering Supervisory Excellence**.*

Books

1. **The First-Time Manager** by Jim McCormick
   A practical guide for new supervisors covering essential skills like delegation, communication, and performance management.

2. **The Leadership GPS: Guiding Your Team to Excellence** by Elijah M. James.
   A must-read for leaders at all levels.

3. **Crucial Conversations: Tools for Talking When Stakes Are High** by Kerry Patterson, Joseph Grenny, Ron McMillan, and Al Switzler
   A must-read for mastering the art of difficult conversations in the workplace.

4. **Leaders Eat Last: Why Some Teams Pull Together and Others Don't** by Simon Sinek
   Explores the importance of creating a supportive and trust-filled workplace culture.

5. **Drive: The Surprising Truth About What Motivates Us** by Daniel H. Pink
   Insights into fostering motivation and engagement within your team.

6. **Radical Candor: Be a Kick-Ass Boss Without Losing Your Humanity** by Kim Scott
   Offers a framework for providing direct feedback while maintaining strong relationships.

Articles and Research Papers

1. **"The Role of Emotional Intelligence in Leadership"**
   Harvard Business Review article exploring the importance of emotional intelligence in effective supervision.

2. **"Managing Remote Teams: Best Practices"**
   A McKinsey & Company report on building productive and engaged hybrid and remote teams.

3. **"The Science of Building High-Performing Teams"**
   Published in the MIT Sloan Management Review, this article delves into evidence-based strategies for team leadership.

Podcasts

1. **"Coaching for Leaders"**
   A podcast offering actionable leadership tips for supervisors at all experience levels.

2. **"HBR IdeaCast"**
   Produced by the Harvard Business Review, this podcast features interviews with thought leaders on leadership and management.

3. "WorkLife with Adam Grant"

Focuses on improving workplace dynamics and fostering innovation within teams.

Websites and Online Tools

1. Society for Human Resource Management (SHRM)

Website: www.shrm.org

Offers a wealth of resources on supervisory practices, legal compliance, and team development.

2. MindTools

Website: www.mindtools.com

Provides tutorials, articles, and tools for leadership, communication, and problem-solving skills.

Workshops and Training Programs

1. Dale Carnegie Leadership Training

Focuses on practical leadership techniques to inspire and empower teams.

2. Leadership Development Programs by Gallup

Emphasizes strengths-based leadership and team engagement strategies.

3. Crucial Conversations Training

Workshops designed to enhance communication and conflict resolution skills.

Assessment Tools

1. DISC Personality Assessment

A tool to understand team members' work styles and improve collaboration.

2. **StrengthsFinder 2.0**

   An assessment to help supervisors and their teams identify and leverage their strengths.

Videos and Webinars

1. **"How Great Leaders Inspire Action" by Simon Sinek (TED Talk)**

   Explores the importance of leading with purpose and building trust.

2. **"The Power of Vulnerability" by Brené Brown (TED Talk)**

   A compelling talk on authenticity and leadership.

3. **"Future of Work: Preparing for the Next Generation of Supervisors"**

   Webinar series by the World Economic Forum addressing upcoming challenges in the workplace.

Support Networks and Professional Organizations

1. **Toastmasters International**

   Develop public speaking and leadership skills in a supportive group setting.

2. **LinkedIn Groups for Supervisors**

   Join groups like *Supervisory and Leadership Excellence* for peer support and insights.

3. **Local Chamber of Commerce Leadership Programs**

   Many chambers offer leadership training programs for supervisors and managers.

APPENDIX C
SELF-ASSESSMENT
QUESTIONNAIRE ON
ETHICAL LEADERSHIP

Take a moment to reflect on your leadership practices. Rate yourself on a scale of 1 to 5 for each statement, where:
1 = Strongly Disagree, 2 = Disagree, 3 = Neutral, 4 = Agree, 5 = Strongly Agree

Ethical Leadership Practices

1. I communicate openly and honestly with my team, even in difficult situations. [ ]

2. I treat all team members fairly and consistently, avoiding favoritism. [ ]

3. I take responsibility for my decisions and actions. [ ]

4. I encourage my team to voice concerns without fear of retaliation. [ ]

5. I model the values and ethical standards I expect from my team. [ ]

6. I make decisions based on what is right, not what is convenient. [ ]

7. I actively promote transparency and accountability within my team. [ ]

8. I address ethical concerns or misconduct promptly and effectively. [ ]

9. I provide clear guidance and training on ethical expectations. [ ]

10. I recognize and reward ethical behavior among team members. [ ]

Reflection

- **Score 40-50:** You exhibit strong ethical leadership and are a role model for your team.

- **Score 30-39:** You demonstrate ethical behavior but may have areas for improvement.

- **Score below 30:** Consider prioritizing ethical leadership development to enhance your impact.

APPENDIX D
GLOSSARY

A

Accountability: the obligation of individuals or teams to take ownership of their actions, decisions, and outcomes, ensuring transparency and responsibility.

Active Listening: a communication skill where the listener fully concentrates on, understands, and thoughtfully responds to the speaker, fostering trust and clarity.

Agility: the capacity to adapt quickly to changing circumstances, solve problems innovatively, and maintain productivity during transitions.

Alignment: the process of ensuring that team goals and individual actions support the organization's broader mission and objectives.

Authenticity: the quality of being genuine, transparent, and consistent in actions and communication, building trust and credibility in leadership.

B

Behavioral Feedback: a feedback method that focuses on specific, observable actions rather than personal traits, promoting constructive growth.

Boundary Setting: establishing clear professional and personal limits to define acceptable behaviors, responsibilities, and expectations within a team.

Burnout: a state of emotional, mental, and physical exhaustion caused by prolonged stress, often affecting productivity and well-being.

C

Change Management: a structured approach to transitioning individuals, teams, and organizations from a current state to a desired future state.

Collaboration: the act of working cooperatively with others, leveraging diverse skills and perspectives to achieve shared goals.

Compassionate Leadership: leading with empathy, understanding, and a genuine concern for the well-being of team members.

Conflict Mediation: a process of resolving disputes by facilitating open communication between conflicting parties to reach a mutually acceptable solution.

Core Values: the fundamental principles that guide behavior and decision-making within an organization.

Critical Thinking: the ability to objectively analyze information, evaluate options, and make reasoned decisions.

D

Decision-Making Framework: a structured approach for evaluating alternatives and making choices, often involving analysis, prioritization, and consultation.

Delegation Matrix: a tool to determine the appropriate tasks for delegation based on the complexity of the task and the competencies of team members.

Difficult Conversations: challenging discussions that require tact, clarity, and emotional intelligence to address sensitive or complex issues effectively.

E

Eisenhower Matrix: a prioritization tool that categorizes tasks into four quadrants based on urgency and importance, helping leaders focus on what matters most.

Empathy: the capacity to understand and share the feelings of others, fostering strong interpersonal relationships and trust.

Empowerment: providing employees with the authority, resources, and confidence to make decisions and take initiative.

Equity: the fair distribution of resources, opportunities, and treatment to ensure that all individuals can thrive, taking into account different needs and circumstances.

Ethical Dilemma: a situation where a leader must choose between conflicting ethical principles or values, requiring careful judgment.

Extrinsic Motivation: drive that comes from external factors such as more money or better working conditions.

F

Facilitation: the process of guiding group discussions or activities to ensure participation, collaboration, and productive outcomes.

Feedback Sandwich: a feedback technique that starts with positive feedback, addresses areas for improvement, and concludes with another positive comment, softening criticism and promoting receptiveness.

Flexible Work Arrangements: alternative schedules or work locations that accommodate employee needs, such as remote work, compressed workweeks, or job sharing.

G

Goal Alignment: ensuring individual, team, and organizational objectives are in harmony, fostering a unified effort toward success.

Growth Mindset: a belief that skills and abilities can be developed through effort, learning, and perseverance.

H

High-Performance Team: a cohesive group that consistently achieves exceptional results through strong collaboration, trust, and accountability.

Human-Centered Leadership: an approach to leadership that prioritizes the needs, well-being, and motivations of team members.

I

Inclusive Leadership: a leadership style that values and leverages diversity, creating an environment where all team members feel respected and empowered.

Influence: the ability to inspire, persuade, or guide others to achieve desired outcomes.

Innovation: the process of creating and implementing new ideas, methods, or solutions to improve organizational performance.

Integrity: adherence to moral and ethical principles, ensuring honesty and transparency in all actions and decisions.

Intrinsic Motivation: drive that comes from internal factors, such as personal satisfaction or the desire to grow, rather than external rewards.

J

Job Enrichment: the process of enhancing a role by adding meaningful responsibilities, opportunities for growth, or increased autonomy.

Judgment: the ability to make sound decisions by evaluating information and weighing potential outcomes.

K

Key Performance Indicators (KPIs): specific metrics used to assess the effectiveness, efficiency, and success of an individual, team, or organization in meeting objectives.

Knowledge Sharing: the practice of exchanging information, skills, and expertise to foster learning and innovation within a team or organization.

L

Leadership Pipeline: a structured process for identifying and developing future leaders within an organization.

Laissez-Faire Leadership: a hands-off leadership style where supervisors delegate decision-making to employees while providing minimal guidance.

Listening Culture: an organizational environment where active listening and open communication are encouraged at all levels.

M

Micromanagement: a supervisory approach characterized by excessive control and attention to detail, often undermining employee autonomy.

Mindfulness: the practice of maintaining awareness of one's thoughts, emotions, and surroundings, enhancing focus and emotional regulation.

N

Negotiation: a collaborative process in which two or more parties work toward a mutually beneficial agreement.

Networking: building and maintaining professional relationships to exchange information, advice, and opportunities.

O

Onboarding: the structured process of integrating new employees into an organization and providing them with the tools and information needed to succeed.

Organizational Culture: the shared values, beliefs, and norms that shape how work is performed and how employees interact within a company.

P

Performance Review: a formal process where a supervisor evaluates an employee's job performance, providing feedback and setting future goals.

Psychological Safety: a team environment where individuals feel secure to express ideas, take risks, and admit mistakes without fear of negative repercussions.

R

Resilience: the ability to recover and adapt effectively in the face of challenges, setbacks, or adversity.

Root Cause Analysis: a problem-solving method, such as the 5 Whys Technique, that identifies the underlying cause of an issue to prevent recurrence.

S

Situational Leadership: a flexible leadership style that adapts to the specific needs of individuals and tasks, balancing direction and support.

Strategic Thinking: the process of anticipating opportunities, challenges, and trends to make informed long-term decisions.

T

Team Cohesion: the level of trust, collaboration, and unity among team members working toward common goals.

Transparency: open and honest communication between supervisors and employees to foster trust and accountability.

V

Visionary Leadership: a leadership style focused on inspiring and guiding a team toward a compelling, long-term vision.

Virtual Team: a team that collaborates primarily through digital tools and remote communication.

W

Wellness Programs: organizational initiatives that support employee well-being, addressing physical, mental, and emotional health.

Workforce Analytics: the use of data to analyze workforce trends, improve decision-making, and enhance organizational performance.

Z

Zero-Tolerance Policy: a strict policy that does not permit certain behaviors, such as harassment or discrimination, in the workplace.

www.ingramcontent.com/pod-product-compliance
Lightning Source LLC
Chambersburg PA
CBHW040850210326
41597CB00029B/4792